The
Life of Victory

By
Meade MacGuire
Young People's Evangelist

TEACH Services, Inc.
Brushton, New York

2007 08 09 10 11 12 · 5 4 3 2 1

Published by

TEACH Services, Inc.
www.TEACHServices.com

CONTENTS

CROWN OR CRUCIFY

I STOOD alone at the bar of God,
  In the hush of the twilight dim,
And faced the question that pierced my heart:
  " What will you do with Him? "
" Crowned or crucified — which shall it be? "
No other choice was offered to me.

I looked on the face so marred with tears
  That were shed in His agony.
The look in His kind eyes broke my heart, —
  'Twas full of love for me.
" The crown or the cross," it seemed to say;
" For or against Me — choose thou today."

He held out His loving hands to me,
  While He pleadingly said, " Obey.
Make Me thy choice, for I love thee so; "
  And I could not say Him nay.
Crowned, not crucified, — this must it be;
No other way was open to me.

I knelt in tears at the feet of Christ,
  In the hush of the twilight dim,
And all that I was, or hoped, or thought,
  Surrendered unto Him.
Crowned, not crucified, — my heart shall know
No king but Christ, who loveth me so.

                        — *Florence E. Johnson.*

The Need of Victory

MUCH is being said these days concerning the victorious life, and with so much preaching, praying, and discussion, the question arises, Why do so few seem to experience complete deliverance from sin and the joy and satisfaction such freedom is said to produce? Why is it that many who really love God and desire earnestly to walk with Him, manifest and confess an utter lack of power to do it? Why do others who have enjoyed a genuine and happy experience, fall back into habits and practices once forsaken, and in their life deny their profession, though they do not give it up?

Why is it that devoted Christians confess their sorrow over habitual sins of impatience, selfishness, pride, criticism, and love of the world, though they profess to believe what the Scriptures say, " He shall save His people from their sins "? Why do some rejoice in the fact that they have victory over great sins, but are constantly defeated by little ones? Is it not strange that Christ can save from the big sins, but cannot save from those they regard as comparatively small? Only recently a young man said, " Week after week I hear earnest pro-

5

fessors of religion confess their defeat and failure. I can do as well without making a profession. Therefore I have no desire to be a Christian, nor any intention of ever becoming one."

Is it not deplorable that Christian people, instead of testifying to the world that Christ saves them from their sins, should publicly bear witness that He does not save them? What hope has the church of attracting sinners to a Saviour whom the church members acknowledge does not save them? Can any one deny that these are fundamental and intensely vital questions?

Three things are essential to a really satisfactory Christian life:

COURAGE — One can be neither happy nor helpful who is discouraged. And one cannot be filled with courage who is conscious of defeat and condemnation. Courage abounds in the heart of him who through Christ is victorious over sin.

POWER — Paul speaks of a class who have " a form of godliness," but deny " the power thereof." The very name " Christian " implies power to live a godly life. To practise sin means to acknowledge weakness and failure, but victory means power.

JOY — The Christian life is to be a fruitful life. This is the test of its success or failure.

But one of the greatest essentials to fruitfulness in the Christian life is the exhibition of joy that attracts and wins to Christ. How can one experience overflowing joy while continually defeated by sin?

So these three great essentials — courage, power, joy — can be experienced fully only in the life that is victorious over sin. Apparently many do not understand what the Scriptures teach concerning the need and the possibility of victory.

The fifth chapter of Romans speaks of the experience of justification by faith in Christ and peace with God. This means deliverance from the guilt and condemnation of sin. The seventh chapter describes the man who has believed in Christ for the remission of sins that are past. He delights in the law of God and hates evil, yet he is bound by a law in his very being which compels him to violate the law he loves, and to do the things he hates.

It is not a question of justification and deliverance from wrath and the condemnation of the law. This has been dealt with in the preceding chapters. It is evident that the man who has been justified needs yet another deliverance from the law of sin and death which is in his members. Without this he is powerless to do the good he longs to do, or to refrain from

the evil he hates; for he says, " To will is present
with me; but how to perform that which is good
I find not."

Many make this discovery in their own experience, and are greatly perplexed. They supposed that when their sins were forgiven and
the love and joy of God filled their hearts, the
conflict with sin must be about finished; but
in truth it had scarcely begun. When the real
secret of victory is discovered, it is so simple
and plain that the glad believer usually cries
out, " Why have I not seen and understood this
before? " How many there are everywhere who,
like the writer of the following words, have long
groped in darkness and defeat, seeking in vain
that which is so freely provided?

" For the first time I have found rest of soul,
because for the first time I have the assurance
that Jesus has come into my heart. Why is it
that I have been so slow in getting this experience? I have needed it so much, and have
longed and prayed and pleaded for it. I have
studied and thought much about it, and discussed it with others, and knew there was a
reality to it. I doubt if many made a more
complete surrender than I, and yet others seemed
contented and satisfied with their Christian experience while doing things which my conscience
would not permit at all. It has been a tre-

mendous struggle with me ever since I gave my heart to the Lord in childhood."

We need victory for Christ's sake, because a sinner really saved from sin is the evidence that His plan of redemption is a success.

We need victory for the sake of other men, for we can have little power to win men to a Saviour whom we acknowledge has not saved us.

We need victory for our own sake; for " the wages of sin is death," and if we keep on sinning, we must expect to receive the wages.

But we need not despair. The inspired Word says, " Thanks be to God, which giveth us the victory."

Let us enter upon a prayerful study of this important subject, with the solemn affirmation in our hearts, Thanks be to God, *I can have the victory.*

And Yet You're Sinning Still

WHEN Moses led his people from Egypt's sunny plain,
From bondage sore and grievous, from hardship, toil,
    and pain,
They soon began to murmur against the sovereign will;
Forgetting God's deliverance, we find them sinning still.
When Moses on the mountain had talked with God alone,
Receiving His commandments on tables made of stone,
The people brought their jewels, the sacrifice did kill,
The golden calf they worshiped, and kept on sinning still.

How often when your dear ones were lying near to death,
You earnestly entreated with every passing breath,
O Father, spare my darling, and I will do Thy will! "
Your prayer was heard and answered, and yet you're
    sinning still.

When sickness overtook you, when sorely racked with
    pain,
You said if God would spare you, you'd bear the cross
    again;
He gave you strength of body, He gave you strength of
    will,
But you forgot your promise, and you are sinning still.

How graciously the Saviour has lengthened out your
    days!
His mercy, never ending, is guiding all your ways.
O brother, heed the warning, your broken vows fulfill,
Lest death should overtake you, and find you sinning still.
Oh, flee the wrath impending, and learn His gracious will,
Lest Jesus, coming quickly, should find you sinning still!

                              — J. G. Dailey.

The Awful Nature of Sin

THE Scripture says, " All have sinned," and, " The wages of sin is death." Our only hope, therefore, is in the atonement of Christ, who took our place as the sinner, received the wages, and met the demands of the violated law.

We can never appreciate the wonders of atoning grace unless we understand the awful nature and ravages of the evil which made the atonement necessary.

Many have a very limited and inadequate conception of sin. When a definition of sin is asked for, the answer is usually given in the language of 1 John 3:4: " Whosoever committeth sin transgresseth also the law: for sin is the transgression of the law." A man who violates the just and necessary civil law of the land is a criminal. He is in rebellion against the best interests of the government and of his fellow men. He does not deserve pity and sympathy, but punishment. So one who transgresses the perfect and holy law of God is a moral criminal. He is in rebellion not only against the authority of God, but against His purity and holiness and goodness.

11

This rebellion is lawlessness. That is why it is the law that reveals sin. No government can tolerate lawlessness. It must be punished, and the penalty for the violation of a perfect law must be in proportion to the seriousness of the transgression. For example, the just punishment for killing another man's sheep would not be equal to the just punishment for killing his child. The consequences of violating the divine law are inconceivably dreadful, therefore the penalty must be proportionately terrible. So the wages of sin is death. The sinner has forfeited his right to life for all eternity. Christ, as man's substitute and redeemer, took the penalty of the law, and thus reconciled man to God and made eternal life possible for him again.

This is the aspect of sin most commonly understood and discussed. But there are other aspects of this terrible evil which it is equally important for us to understand, and without which we shall not adequately appreciate the matchless love of God and the wonders of Christ's atoning sacrifice.

In Isaiah 1:16 we read, "Wash you, make you clean; put away the evil of your doings from before Mine eyes."

This scripture represents sin as a moral defilement that needs to be cleansed. So it continues in verse 18, " Come now, and let us reason together, saith the Lord: though your sins be as scarlet, they shall be as white as snow; though they be red like crimson, they shall be as wool." Before man sinned, he was pure and holy, and, like the angels, rejoiced in fellowship and association with God. Now his uncleanness and impurity unfit him for coming into God's presence.

" We are all as an unclean thing, and all our righteousnesses are as filthy rags; and we all do fade as a leaf; and our iniquities, like the wind, have taken us away." Isa. 64: 6. This uncleanness may be sin in the inner life, in the heart, or it may be in the outer life, in the conduct. Both of these are illustrated in the ceremonial laws of defilement and cleansing given in Leviticus and Numbers.

The defilement of the leper was a type of the moral impurity of sin within. The defilement from contact with a corpse was a type of moral impurity in the outer life or contact with the world. The ceremonial laws provided complete and adequate cleansing from all ceremonial defilement within and without. This represents the fact that God cannot and will not tolerate sin in any form, and has made full and adequate provision for cleansing and keeping from its impurity.

We must therefore see in Jesus not only the one who took our place as a criminal, and suffered the just penalty of a violated law, but the one whose shed blood cleanses and purifies us from the awful pollution and filth of sin in the soul.

Still another aspect of sin is suggested in Luke 5 : 30-32 : " Their scribes and Pharisees murmured against His disciples, saying, Why do ye eat and drink with publicans and sinners? And Jesus answering said unto them, They that are whole need not a physician; but they that are sick. I came not to call the righteous, but sinners to repentance."

Sin is a sickness of the soul, and there are many forms of *sin-sickness*. As the physical body suffers from many forms of disease, so the soul suffers from corresponding spiritual maladies. As there is physical blindness, deafness, paralysis, anemia, stupor, and deformity, so in the spiritual life all these ailments occur. Jesus came as the Great Physician, not for the benefit of those who are whole, but for those who are sick. So it was written of Him, " Unto you that fear My name shall the Sun of Righteousness arise with healing in His wings." Mal. 4 : 2. " He healeth the broken in heart, and bindeth up their wounds." Ps. 147 : 3. " He was wounded for our transgressions, He was bruised for our iniquities: the chastisement of our peace was upon Him; and with His stripes we are healed." Isa. 53:5.

This aspect of sin as a spiritual malady requiring healing is most strikingly presented in Matthew 13:15: "This people's heart is waxed gross, and their ears are dull of hearing, and their eyes they have closed; lest at any time they should see with their eyes, and hear with their ears, and should understand with their heart, and should be converted, and I should heal them."

It is sin that makes men spiritually deaf and dumb — robbed of their sensitiveness to the presence and voice of God, and of their power to praise and pray. But God in His tender mercy pleads with men, " Return, ye backsliding children, and I will heal your backslidings." Jer. 3:22. "I will restore health unto thee, and I will heal thee of thy wounds, saith the Lord." Jer. 30:17. "Who His own self bare our sins in His own body on the tree, that we, being dead to sins, should live unto righteousness: by whose stripes ye were healed." 1 Peter 2:24.

Christ's death meets the demands of a broken law. His blood cleanses from the defilement and impurity of sin. His power heals the wounds and diseases and deformities sin has caused.

The Scripture presents sin in another aspect as a ruling power. It takes possession of our will, and thus becomes master, and we its servants. It sits on the throne of our lives, reigning over us, and holding us captives and slaves.

"Jesus answered them, Verily, verily, I say unto you, Whosoever committeth sin is the servant of sin." John 8:34.

"Know ye not, that to whom ye yield yourselves servants to obey, his servants ye are to whom ye obey; whether of sin unto death, or of obedience unto righteousness?" Rom. 6:16.

From this terrible mastery of sin Christ came to deliver men. His power alone can set us free from the slavery of sinful habits and passions. Of Him it was written, "The Lord . . . hath sent Me to bind up the broken-hearted, to proclaim liberty to the captives, and the opening of the prison to them that are bound." Isa. 61:1. "If the Son therefore shall make you free, ye shall be free indeed." John 8:36. "Sin shall not have dominion over you: for ye are not under the law, but under grace." Rom. 6:14. "Who hath delivered us from the power of darkness." Col. 1:13.

Still another aspect of sin is set forth strikingly in Romans: "To will is present with me; but how to perform that which is good I find not. For the good that I would I do not: but

the evil which I would not, that I do. . . . I find
then a *law*, that, when I would do good, evil is
present with me. For I delight in the law of
God after the inward man: but I see *another
law in my members,* warring against the law of
my mind, and bringing me into captivity to the
law of sin which is in my members." Rom.
7 : 18-23.

Here it is described as "a law," "another law
in my members," "the law of sin."

The Bible makes a distinction between sin
and sins. Sins are acts of transgression, sin is
an inherited tendency or law of our being.

There is an important lesson suggested in
Romans 7 : 18, that many are slow to learn. "I
know that in me (that is in my flesh) dwelleth
no good thing."

Is it all or only a part of me that has fallen
under sin and is rebellious, impure, sick, and in
slavery to evil? To learn that I am all bad and
that there is no good thing in me, is one of the
greatest steps toward appreciation of the atonement of Christ.

Paul says, "To will is present with me; but
how to perform that which is good I find not."
Rom. 7 : 18.

This is because of the law of sin which is in
my members. There is only one means of deliverance from this inherent law of sin. That is

Christ. He took humanity upon Him. He con-
quered sin while in a body which had come
under the hereditary law of sin. He now proposes to live that same sinless life in my members. His presence completely counteracts the
power of the law of sin. So Paul says in Romans
8 : 2, " The law of the Spirit of life in Christ
Jesus hath made me free from the law of sin and
death."

From the condemnation of sin as an offense
against God, Christ frees us. From the defilement of sin He cleanses us. From the sickness
and deformity of sin He heals us. From the
slavery of sin He delivers us. From the law of
sin He frees us. All this He does for us by His
death and by His indwelling presence.

" I DARE not work my soul to save,
That work the Lord has done;
But I will work like any slave
For love of God's dear Son."

How Can God Justify a Sinner?

IT is an interesting fact that somewhere in the Bible we find a full presentation, at least once, of each essential doctrine. In John 3 is discussed the doctrine of the new birth; in Isaiah 53, the vicarious atonement; in John 14 to 17, the Holy Spirit; in Matthew 24, the second advent; in 1 Corinthians 15, the resurrection; in 1 John 4, love; in Hebrews 11, faith; and we might add many more to the list.

The great doctrine of justification by faith is presented most fully and explicitly in Romans 1:16 to 5:11. Following this, in chapters 5:12 to 8:39, we have an equally clear and exhaustive presentation of the victorious life in Christ. As justification necessarily precedes sanctification, it will be well for us to examine carefully the foundation upon which the latter is built.

"I am not ashamed of the gospel of Christ: for it is the power of God unto salvation to every one that believeth; to the Jew first, and also to the Greek. For therein is the righteousness of God revealed." Rom. 1:16, 17.

Many are interested in the gospel as the unfolding of a plan to save the lost, who never

19

think of it as first of all a revelation of the righteousness of God in saving sinners, though this is the keystone to the whole arch of redemption.

A man is brought into court charged with having incurred large debts which he does not pay. He may declare that he cannot pay, and may give as reasons that he has been unfortunate or sick or has been defrauded by others. But the law demands payment, and if he cannot produce the money, judgment is rendered against him. The law holds him guilty. On the other hand, if some friend comes forward and pays all the obligations, the man is immediately acquitted. The law demands the full amount, and the judge is responsible for the infliction of the just penalty. But as soon as the debts are paid, the man is free, the law is upheld, and the judge has done his duty.

When sin entered the world, the sentence of death was passed upon all men by the divine law. As the first step in the plan of redemption, God must devise a way by which He can honorably acquit the guilty sinner. How can the debt be paid? It was impossible for man to atone for his own sin. How can God remain righteous, and justify the unrighteous? This was the baffling problem introduced by sin, which nothing but the infinite wisdom and love of God could ever solve. Any announcement of a plan of salvation for sinners must make plain how God can maintain His righteousness, and yet the debt be paid and the ungodly justified.

In many places in the Scriptures the inspired penman has portrayed the awful consequences of the fall, or succession of falls, by which man has become so corrupt and degraded. There are really two great themes which run like mountain ranges through the pages of sacred revelation. They are the awful fact of sin, and the wonderful fact of divine love and redemption. It is necessary to realize the terrible nature and ravages of sin in order to appreciate the plan of salvation. One does not long for a remedy for his disease until he becomes conscious that he is sick, nor can he appreciate such a remedy. It is therefore futile and inconsistent to present a remedy for the sin-sick and lost without a clear description of the disease of sin, its cause and its consequences.

A great deal of modern preaching leaves out the old-fashioned doctrine of sin, with its awful depravity and ruin, and so has little use for the old-fashioned gospel of salvation through the atonement of Christ, by which sins are washed away in His precious blood.

But the record in God's Word stands, and its vivid pictures paint the character of men today

as faithfully as they did fifty generations ago.
Jude describes the sinners of Sodom and Gomor-
rah. He calls them " filthy dreamers," and men-
tions their " hard speeches " and their " ungodly
deeds." Thus degraded in mind, in conversation, and in actions, they defied Heaven, and
brought upon themselves the " vengeance of
eternal fire."

The wise man said, " Lo, this only have I
found, that God hath made man upright; but
they have sought out many inventions." Eccl.
7: 29. So Paul in Galatians 5 gives a list of
seventeen forms of the terrible disease of sin.

Perhaps the darkest picture of all is given in
Romans 1: 21-32. By gazing upon the awful
ruin and desolation sin has wrought, the mind
may more fully appreciate the length and
breadth and depth and height of redeeming love
revealed in the chapters following. In this
passage the spiritual, moral, and physical degradation are fearlessly exposed, that men, seeing
in this divine mirror their inmost lives, may
bow in conscious guilt and shame before God.
It is made very emphatic that " all have sinned,
and come short of the glory of God." Rom.
3: 23. " For we have before proved both Jews
and Gentiles, that they are all under sin."
Verse 9. " Now we know that what things soever
the law saith, it saith to them who are under

the law; that every mouth may be stopped, and all the world may become guilty before God." Verse 19.

In Romans 2: 13 he says, "Not the hearers of ? law are just before God, but the doers of the ˚ shall be justified." Then he proceeds to ᴠ that *there are no doers of the law,* but all ? violated its precepts and are guilty, which gs the inevitable conclusion, "Therefore by deeds of the law shall no flesh be justified ʟis sight." Rom. 3: 20.

ʳe need to understand the distinction be- tᴡ ᴇn "just" and "justified." If we call a man ju , we refer to his character; if justified, we refer to his standing. An unjust man, if legally tried on some charge and acquitted, is justified and accounted and treated as though innocent.

In the strictest sense a sinner never can be just, but Christ, the just one, took the sinner's place, so that God could put the repentant sinner in Christ's place, and declare him justified.

All men had sinned, and were sentenced to death by the divine law. That law was perfect and holy, and justice demanded its execution. But a loving and merciful God longed to rescue the sinner. The great problem was how God could pardon the sinner and save him from the penalty without either setting aside the divine law or sharing in the guilt of the transgressor. No human mind could ever have solved so difficult a problem.

A holy God has made a perfect law, designed to safeguard the highest interests of the universe forever. So long as His government stands, the law must be maintained. The moment the certainty of punishment for disobedience and rebellion ceases, there is an end of the government. It will not do for God to save the sinner at the expense of His character or His government.

With wonder and gratitude we consider the divine plan which substitutes God's Son for the sinner, before the law. Being born of woman, He identified Himself with the human race. Through the mercy of God the sinner and the Saviour actually exchange places. Christ becomes the sinner, is condemned, and dies. The sinner is adopted as a son, justified and declared holy. By Christ's life of perfect obedience to the law and His vicarious death, the ends of the law and justice are fully met, so that God can judicially acquit the sinner, and still maintain His own righteousness and the integrity of His law.

What would have been accomplished had the law taken its course, and its penalty been visited upon guilty man?

1. The law would have been vindicated and exalted before the universe.

2. The awful character and results of sin would have been exposed.

3. Just punishment would have been meted to violators of a holy law.

4. The love of God would have been vindicated in protecting the universe.

5. Provision would have been made for the extermination of sin.

6. The law would have been maintained at any cost.

It is plain that all these purposes were fully accomplished in the substitutionary death of Christ. So the gospel must stand first of all upon this principle,— that God is righteous, though He justifies the unrighteous. Paul says Christ is set forth to do two things,—" to be a propitiation through faith in His blood," and " to declare His righteousness." Rom. 3 : 25. To emphasize this thought he repeats, " To declare, I say, at this time His righteousness: that He might be just, and the justifier of him which believeth in Jesus." Verse 26.

Here the great principle stands forth clearly. All have sinned, and can never be justified by the law which has been violated, for it only condemns. But God has given His Son as an atoning sacrifice, not to evade the law or set it aside, but to declare His righteousness in the remission of sins. This, then, is the purpose of the atonement, to make it possible for God to remain holy and just, and yet not only pardon the sinner, but account him just, acquitting him of guilt, and giving him the standing of one who has not sinned.

"It was possible for Adam, before the fall, to form a righteous character by obedience to God's law. But he failed to do this, and because of his sin our natures are fallen, and we cannot make ourselves righteous. Since we are sinful, unholy, we cannot perfectly obey a holy law. We have no righteousness of our own with which to meet the claims of the law of God. But Christ has made a way of escape for us. He lived on earth amid trials and temptations such as we have to meet. He lived a sinless life. He died for us, and now He offers to take our sins and give us His righteousness. If you give yourself to Him, and accept Him as your Saviour, then, sinful as your life may have been, for His sake you are accounted righteous. Christ's character stands in place of your character, and you are accepted before God just as if you had not sinned." — "*Steps to Christ*," *p. 62* (*pocket edition*).

How Can a Sinner Secure Justification?

WE have been studying the wonderful plan God devised, which enables Him not only to pardon, but to justify a sinner. The sinner then stands before the law free from fear and condemnation, as though he had never sinned.

"It is our privilege to go to Jesus and be cleansed, and to stand before the law without shame or remorse."—"*Steps to Christ,*" *p. 5.*

But the question arises, What must the sinner do to secure this justification? Has God made any condition which man must meet, and without which he remains under condemnation?

It is the duty of a judge, when dealing with criminals, to mete out exact and impartial justice. But had God visited exact justice on all sinners, they would have been destroyed. Sometimes there are reasons why a judge might desire very much to show mercy to the transgressor. It may be his own son who has gone astray and violated the law. In order to maintain law and justice and good government, the judge must inflict just and legal punishment upon his own son, the same as upon any other criminal. If

27

he were to extend mercy, there would need to be
some good and adequate reason which would
justify him in the eyes of his fellow men.

God longed to extend mercy to His erring
children, and He provided a way by which they
might be pardoned and justified. But this plan
includes a condition on man's part, which justifies God in the eyes of the universe.

Our heavenly Father glories in His own disposition to show mercy. When Moses prayed
to see God's glory, the answer was: " I will
make all My goodness pass before thee, and I
will proclaim the name of the Lord before thee."
" And the Lord passed by before him, and proclaimed, The Lord, The Lord God, *merciful* and
gracious, long-suffering, and abundant in goodness and truth." Ex. 33 : 19 ; 34 : 6.

The first attribute which God gives in His
own name is " merciful." His name stands for
His character. While He is absolutely just, He
is also infinitely merciful.

Mercy is a disposition to pardon the guilty.
Justice treats the transgressor as he deserves.
Mercy sets aside the penalty, and treats him
better than he deserves. Mercy is exercised,
then, only where there is guilt. There is no
need of mercy unless the penalty of the law has
been incurred. No one therefore would expect
or desire mercy unless he was conscious that he

had transgressed and deserved punishment. So long as one believes himself innocent, he demands justice, but never asks for mercy.

A man has burned a valuable building, and is arrested and brought to trial. A friend has taken pity on him, and offered to pay the damages. But the criminal brazenly declares his innocence, and demands justice. Surely the judge could not extend mercy and set aside the penalty.

Is it not plain that although God gave His Son to die for our sins and pay the debt, He cannot extend mercy unless we recognize our guilt and seek for mercy?

David says, " I trust in the mercy of God forever and ever." Ps. 52: 8. When a sinner cries for mercy, this implies that he recognizes his guilt and merited condemnation, and has no hope in justice. Justice would mean his destruction, so he casts himself wholly upon the mercy of God.

We should not confuse mercy with grace, or favor. God shows grace toward all, both good and bad. But exact justice will finally be meted out to those who do not earnestly seek God for mercy.

The Saviour taught us to hope in the mercy of God. " The publican, standing afar off, would not lift up so much as his eyes unto heaven, but smote upon his breast, saying, God be *merciful* to me a sinner. I tell you, this man went down to his house justified." Luke 18:13, 14.

God justified the sinner who cried to Him for mercy.

Let us be sure we understand all that is involved in this prayer for mercy. The man acknowledges:

1. That he is a guilty sinner.
2. That the law he has transgressed is just and righteous.
3. That he deserves only punishment.
4. That God would be just in visiting the penalty upon him.
5. That he believes God is merciful.
6. That his only hope is in the mercy of God.

Many do not seem to understand that these principles are the basis for the whole doctrine of repentance and confession.

The exercise of mercy is one of the most delicate phases of a government. There is danger that men will get the impression that it sets aside the law. Mercy only sets aside the penalty. The problem is how the full majesty of the law can be maintained while the execution of the penalty is withdrawn. If mercy is exercised, something must be done to satisfy the demands of justice and sustain the law. However much God may desire to extend mercy, He cannot do it in a way to imperil the law and give license to sin.

So it is plain that no sinner can be justified unless he is willing to repent. Mercy cannot be extended to one in rebellion.

The sinner must acknowledge and confess his sins. God could not be just in the eyes of the universe if He justified one who was in open rebellion against Him. He must have the sinner's testimony against himself and in favor of the law and obedience. This is why confession is necessary. The sinner confesses that he is wrong and that the law he has transgressed is right. He desires to come into harmony with that law. He makes restitution, so far as possible, for the injury he has done to God and his fellow men. He fully determines to reform. Then God can extend pardon and justification.

One who does not truly repent, confess, and reform, is still arrayed against the government and law of God, and deserves no mercy.

There is no hope for the sinner except in the mercy which meets him prostrate, without excuse or apology, confessing all his guilt, and trusting only in the merits of Christ.

This Hour in Me

"My God! my God! and can it be
   That I should sin so lightly now,
And think no more of evil thoughts
   Than of the wind that waves the bough?

" I sin, and heaven and earth go round
   As if no dreadful deed were done;
As if Thy blood had never flowed
   To hinder sin, or to atone.

" Shall it be always thus, O Lord?
   Wilt Thou not work this hour in me
The grace Thy passion merited,
   Hatred of self, and love of Thee?

" Oh, by the pains of Thy pure love,
   Grant me the gift of holy fear;
And by Thy woes and bloody sweat,
   Oh, wash my guilty conscience clear.

" Ever when tempted make me see,
   Beneath the olives' moon-pierced shade,
My God, alone, outstretched, and bruised,
   And bleeding on the earth He made.

" And make me feel it was my sin,
   As though no other sins there were,
That was to Him who bears the world
   A load that He could scarcely bear."

Delivered by Death

THERE is a great deal of modern preaching which presents, as a remedy for sin, love, social regeneration, culture, self-development, etc. According to the Scriptures, the only way to deal with sin is to begin with death. In the beginning God judged, condemned, and pronounced the sentence of death upon the sinner. That death sentence has never been revoked, and therefore every sinner must die. When a man is born again, there is a new creation. This new man agrees with God in pronouncing the sentence of death upon his old nature, the "old man."

God regards every true disciple as having died and been buried with Christ. Through the outward ceremony of baptism the believer now expresses and typifies his faith in this as a spiritual experience. Not that this death and burial is a historical fact, but like justification, it is a judicial act which God reckons so. In the rite of baptism the believer solemnly agrees with God in thus reckoning.

Throughout the New Testament, the fact that Christ died is the ground for assuming that every true believer died. "Who His own self bare our sins in His own body on the tree, that we, being dead to sins, should live unto righteousness." 1 Peter 2:24. Christ, the Son of man, became one with the sinner, that the sinner might be reckoned one with Christ in that death. The obedience of Christ is counted as the sinner's own, and the sacrifice of Christ as the sinner's satisfaction of the claims of the divine law. God reckons the believer in Christ, and as such, judged, acquitted, and accounted righteous.

"We are buried with Him by baptism into death." Rom. 6:4.

"All Christians died when Christ died. That is the date for all of that death which is their life. But the personal appropriation of this death with Christ is later. It comes only with faith. Our baptism was a sort of funeral, a solemn act of consigning us to that death of Christ in which we are made one with Him. Not that we might remain dead, but that we might rise with Him from death, experience the power of His resurrection, and live the life we now live in the flesh, as men who have already died and have risen again."— *Vaughan.*

"Ye are dead, and your life is hid with Christ in God." Col. 3:3. It is because so many know little of the actual experience of dying in Christ His death, that they find it so difficult to live in Him His life.

What Paul emphatically teaches is that when a man is born again, there is a new life imparted from above. The "old man" which was in slavery to sin is brought to the cross of Christ, and by faith is crucified with Him. In the solemn act of baptism the new man, born from above, consigns the "old man" to the grave. The believer reckons himself as having died to sin and been resurrected to live unto God. Shall he continue in the sins which possessed and controlled the former life? God forbid.

Undoubtedly the great difficulty with the majority of believers is that they are trying to live Christ's life without first having died Christ's death. They seem to have the notion that Christ died so that we need not die, and so through faith in Christ they hope to live without dying. Paul said, "They that are in the flesh *cannot* please God" (Rom. 8:8), and "*they that are Christ's have crucified the flesh*" (Gal. 5:24).

> " If Christ would live and reign in me,
>   I must die;
> With Him I crucified must be;
>   I must die;
> Lord, drive the nails, nor heed the groans,
> My flesh may writhe and make its moans,
> But in this way, and this alone,
>   I must die.

" When I am dead, then, Lord, to Thee
    I shall live;
My time, my strength, my all to Thee
    I shall give.
O may the Son now make me free!
Here, Lord, I give my all to Thee;
For time and for eternity
    I will live."

What is the teaching of the Master?

" Except a corn of wheat fall into the ground and die, it abideth alone: but if it die, it bringeth forth much fruit. He that loveth his life shall lose it; and he that hateth his life in this world shall keep it unto life eternal." John 12: 24, 25.

And again: " Whosoever will come after Me, let him deny himself, and take up his cross, and follow Me. For whosoever will save his life shall lose it; but whosoever shall lose his life for My sake and the gospel's, the same shall save it." Luke 8: 34, 35.

The cross is the symbol of death. When a man goes to the cross, it is the end of that man. Any life he may know later must necessarily be a new life which is not his own. Then he can say with Paul: " I am crucified with Christ: nevertheless I live; yet not I, but Christ liveth in me." Gal. 2: 20. Making this death with Christ actual is the only way into a victorious life with Christ which is actual. *It is very plain from Paul's words that living Christ's life continuously is dependent upon dying with Him daily.*

"Always bearing about in the body the dying of the Lord Jesus, that the life also of Jesus might be made manifest in our body." 2 Cor. 4:10.

It is much more popular these days to talk about life than death, but not more necessary, for death is the way into life. Many have not seen or understood the necessity of this death; and others, having seen it, are afraid or unwilling to die. As the natural man shrinks from the thought of physical death, so "they that are in the flesh" (Rom. 8:8), the carnal man, recoil and struggle against the ordeal of crucifixion. Paul said, "I die daily" (1 Cor. 15:31); and he also said, "Christ liveth in me" (Gal. 2:20). It is the daily dying of self that makes room for the living of Christ.

Let us study with earnest and prayerful hearts the glorious inducements God offers to those who are willing to die that they may live. Let us remember our Master, who, "when the time came that He should be received up, . . . steadfastly set His face to go to Jerusalem" (Luke 9:51), knowing that suffering and death on the cross were awaiting Him.

Again and again it is emphasized in the Scriptures that we enter into life with Christ by first sharing by faith in His death. When we say that we share in Christ's death by faith, we do not mean that it is some mystical or imaginary experience. It is a death as terribly real, in the spiritual realm, as physical death is in the natural realm. It is attended by pangs and suffering and shrinking, and opposed by all the powers and passions of the unregenerate nature. As a mere theory, it avails nothing. It is therefore of greatest importance that the death and burial of the " old man " of sin receive due emphasis.

" Burial is the seal and certificate of death. Christ's interment in the rock-hewn sepulcher gave conclusive evidence of the reality of His death. His enemies said, ' That is the end of another deception; ' while His friends said, ' We trusted that it had been He who should have redeemed Israel.' The phrase, ' buried with Christ,' denotes, then, the absoluteness of our death with Him, as a man who passes away is said to be dead and buried. The relatives and friends of a Hindu convert to Christianity, in order to show how completely they have cast him off, actually celebrate his funeral, and treat him after this open display of his death, as if he really no longer existed."

"Just as we have all known what it is to turn away at last from the grave-side where the body of some loved one has been laid at rest; just as we have lingered to take the last look at the coffin, and have then come away with tear-dimmed eyes, feeling all was over; so they who are really dead and buried with Christ think of that old natural self as having been wrapped in its winding-sheet, and buried in the dark grave with Christ's burial. The old habits, the old besetments, the old sins, are, by a faith that knows nothing of intermittency, completely past and gone."— *Mantle*.

If we will study God's Word, we shall find abundant incentive to face this death, for it must be a voluntary one, and we must go to the cross, as our Master did, of our own free will.

Let us first be clear as to what it is that must die. Paul said, "I am crucified with Christ." Did Paul mean that there was some bad in him and some good, and that the bad was crucified? Manifestly not, for he solemnly declares, "I know that in me . . . dwelleth no good thing." Rom. 7:18. Perhaps the names of this great Bible character may be used as typical of what is meant in this death.

In his early life he was Saul.

Later he was born again. The new man was named Paul. Paul crucified Saul and reckoned him dead. The birth of Paul meant the crucifixion of Saul, and day by day Christ lived in Paul, and Paul crucified Saul.

If these statements seem mysterious and difficult to some, it is because they are unfamiliar with the simple facts regarding the two natures. Saul was born of the Adam nature, and there was no good thing in him. He was the chief of sinners. Paul was born from above, born of the Spirit, a new creature, a partaker of the divine nature.

It is this Adam nature typified by Saul that every man must crucify. "They that are Christ's have crucified the flesh." Gal. 5:24.

In order that this death may be a reality in us, we need first to realize and acknowledge what we are. We are not willing to die until we recognize the fact that we are fit only to die — that we are so vile and unholy that God is just in pronouncing the sentence of death upon us. Then we agree with God in sentencing ourselves to death, and co-operate with Him in making it actual.

Let us examine the teaching of the Scripture concerning this:

"Verily, verily, I say unto you, Except a corn of wheat fall into the ground and die, it abideth alone: but if it die, it bringeth forth much fruit." John 12:24. We understand that Christ was speaking of Himself. But the principle involved He applies to all men.

"He that loveth his life shall lose it; and he that *hateth his life* in this world shall keep it unto life eternal." John 12 : 25. This is a strong expression,— that a man may secure eternal life only by hating his life in this world.

Is it not quite plain, in the light of our previous illustration? Had Saul of Tarsus loved his life, he must have lost it; but Paul, hating and crucifying the Saul life, entered into eternal life.

Why did he hate his life? Because he recognized the fact that in him dwelt no good thing. This is expressed very forcefully in Job 42 : 5, 6 : "I have heard of Thee by the hearing of the ear: but now mine eye seeth Thee. Wherefore *I abhor myself,* and repent in dust and ashes."

There is a still stronger expression in Ezekiel 20 : 43 : "There shall ye remember your ways, and all your doings, wherein ye have been defiled; and *ye shall loathe yourselves* in your sight for all your evils that ye have committed."

These scriptures teach that self is so bad that it is fit only to die. It is utterly corrupted, and so vile and unholy that no part of the Adam nature can be reclaimed. "The carnal mind is enmity against God: for it is not subject to the law of God, neither indeed can be." Rom. 8 : 7.

When a man realizes that his whole being is poisoned with the loathsome, deadly disease of sin, so that there is no good thing in him, he begins to hate himself, to loathe and abhor his nature, which is " deceitful above all things, and desperately wicked " (Jer. 17 : 9), and he longs to die to all this, if by so doing he may enter into a pure and holy life. This is a very essential part of the Saviour's teaching.

" Apart from Thee,
I am not only naught, but worse than naught,
A wretched monster, horrible of mien!
And when I work my works in self's vain strength,
However good and holy they may seem,
These works are hateful — nay, in Thy pure sight
Are criminal and fiendish, since thereby
I seek, and please, and magnify myself
In subtle pride of goodness, and ascribe
To *self* the glory that is Thine alone.
So dark, corrupt, so vile a thing is self.
Seen in the presence of Thy purity,
It turns my soul to loathing and disgust;
Yea, all the virtues that it boasts to own
Are foul and worthless when I look on Thee.
O that there might be no more *I* or *mine!*
That in myself I might no longer own
As mine, my life, my thinking, or my choice,
Or any other motion but in me
That Thou, my God, my Jesus, might be all,
And work the all in all! Let that, O Lord,
Be dumb forever, die, and cease to be,
Which Thou dost not Thyself in me inspire,
And speak and work."

— *Gerhard Tersteegen.*

" Then said Jesus unto His disciples, If any man will come after Me, let him deny himself, and *take up his cross,* and follow Me. For whosoever will save his life shall lose it : and whosoever will *lose his life* for My sake shall save it." Matt. 16 : 24, 25.

In these two verses the expressions, " take up his cross " and " lose his life," are evidently equivalent. And let not the fact be overlooked that in each case it is a voluntary act on the part of men. In the days of Christ, when a man walked down the street bearing a wooden cross, all men knew that he was going to his death, because the cross was the symbol of the death sentence.

When Jesus bore the cross, He acknowledged the death sentence upon the sin nature. He took our nature, the Adam nature, the Saul life, and agreeing with the Father that this nature was fit only to die, He went voluntarily to the cross, and bore that fallen nature to its inevitable and necessary death.

" God sending His own Son in the likeness of sinful flesh, and for sin, condemned sin in the flesh." Rom. 8 : 3.

By this great sacrifice Christ made provision for the death of the Adam nature in you and me, if we are willing to bring this degenerate nature of ours to His cross and nail it there.

On the cross, Christ bore the guilt and penalty for all our transgressions.

" As many as are of the works of the law are under the curse: for it is written, Cursed is every one that continueth not in all things which are written in the book of the law to do them." " Christ hath redeemed us from the curse of the law, being made a curse for us: for it is written, Cursed is every one that hangeth on a tree." Gal. 3: 10, 13.

But even should we obtain pardon through His death, we still have this vile, unholy, degenerate nature which unfits us for fellowship with God.

However, abundant provision has been made for a new nature. " Whereby are given unto us exceeding great and precious promises: that by these ye might be partakers of the divine nature." 2 Peter 1: 4.

So through the atoning death of Christ, provision has been made for man's pardon and justification; and through the ministry of His word, provision is made for the impartation of the divine nature. But one great problem remains, — what is to become of the old degenerate Adam nature? This is what must go to the cross.

This voluntary fellowship with Christ in the sufferings and death of the cross is the gateway into life in and with Christ. Our only hope for deliverance from sin, for holiness and for eternal life, lies in union with Christ, and this union is effected only at the cross. This is why the cross is the very center of the plan of salvation; why " both the redeemed and the unfallen beings will find in the cross of Christ their science and their song."—" *The Desire of Ages,*" *page 20.*

WHAT is the meaning of the Christian life?
   Is it success, or vulgar wealth, or. name?
Is it a weary struggle — a mean strife —
   For rank, low gains, ambition, or for fame?
What sow we for? The world? For fleeting time,
   Or far-off harvests, richer, more sublime?
The brightest life on earth was one of loss;
   The noblest head was wreathed with sharpest thorn.
Has He not consecrated pain — the cross?
   What higher crown can Christian brow adorn?
Be we content to follow on the road
Which men count failure, but which leads to God.
                 — *Unknown.*

SOMETIME

SOMETIME when all life's lessons have been learned,
  And sun and stars forevermore have set,
The things which our weak judgment here has spurned,
  The things o'er which we grieved with lashes wet,
Will flash before us, out of life's dark night,
  As stars shine most in deeper tints of blue;
And we shall see how all God's plans were right,
  And how what seemed reproof was love most true.

And we shall see how, while we frown and sigh,
  God's plans go on as best for you and me;
How, when we called, He heeded not our cry,
  Because His wisdom to the end could see.
And e'en as prudent parents disallow
  Too much of sweet to craving babyhood,
So God, perhaps, is keeping from us now
  Life's sweetest things because it seemeth good.

And if, sometimes, commingled with life's wine,
  We find the wormwood, and rebel and shrink,
Be sure a wiser hand than yours and mine
  Pours out this portion for our lips to drink.
If we could push ajar the gates of life,
  And stand within, and all God's workings see,
We could interpret all this doubt and strife,
  And for each mystery could find a key!

But not today. Then be content, poor heart!
  God's plans, like lilies pure and white unfold;
We must not tear the close-shut leaves apart,
  Time will reveal the chalices of gold.
And if, through patient toil, we reach the land
  Where tired feet, with sandals loosed, may rest,
When we shall clearly know and understand,
  I think that we shall say, " God knew the best! "
                              — *May Riley Smith.*

Alive unto God

As a result of the disobedience of Adam, his whole nature was changed. God had given him a nature pure and upright, and capable of perfect obedience. Now it was impure, unholy, and tending continually to transgress. He could not transmit to his children a nature higher or purer than he possessed, consequently the sentence of death which fell upon him embraced the whole human family.

" Wherefore, as by one man sin entered into the world, and death by sin; and so death passed upon all men, for that all have sinned." Rom. 5 : 12.

When Adam was placed on trial, it was the probation of the human race. When he fell, all were included in the fall; for he stood as the official head and representative of the race. Having fallen, he had no power to regain his lost character and position for himself and his posterity. To redeem the race, Christ the Son of God came to earth, and became the Son of man, in order that He might take the place from which Adam fell as the official head, or representative, of the human family. He endured the test, succeeding where Adam failed. Upon the

cross He paid the penalty for man's transgression, and thus "became the author of eternal salvation unto all them that obey Him."
Heb. 5 : 9.

"And so it is written, the first man Adam was
made a living soul; the last Adam was made a
quickening spirit." "The first man is of the
earth, earthy: the second man is the Lord from
heaven." 1 Cor. 15 : 45, 47.

Here it is stated that Christ is "the second
man" and "the last Adam." The first Adam
fell, and could then represent only a lost race.
The last Adam is the head and representative
of the race He has redeemed. He is the Head
of the new creation. By blood and birth we
are all the children of the first man, the subjects
of the first Adam; by virtue of the atonement of
Christ, we may be born again into the family of
the last Adam. In the first Adam we are dead
in sin; in the last Adam we may die to sin, and
be "alive unto God through Jesus Christ our
Lord." Rom. 6 : 11. All born into the family
of Adam share in his fall; similarly, all born
into the family of Christ share in His death
to sin. So we can understand how God reckons
those who receive Christ to have died when He
died. God looks upon Christ's death as typical
and representative. Just as the children of
Adam fell in Adam's fall, so the children of

Christ died in His death; for He died as the last
Adam, the official representative of the human
race. Therefore Paul says: "We thus judge,
that if one died for all, then were all dead."
2 Cor. 5 : 14.

It is as though Adam should say, "If you are
born into my family, you inherit from me a sinful nature, and therefore come under condemnation of the divine law." And Christ, the last
Adam, says, "If you by the Spirit are born into
My family, you inherit from Me the divine
nature, and therefore are justified by the divine
law."

× The Scripture tells us of two ways in which
we are to regard the cross. It is the basis of our
redemption in Christ, and it is the basis of our
fellowship with Christ. The law pronounced a
condemnation, or curse, upon sin and all that
pertained to it, and so it is written:

"Christ hath redeemed us from the curse of
the law, being made a curse for us: for it is
written, Cursed is every one that hangeth on a
tree." Gal. 3 : 13. So we look to the redemption of the cross as the ground of all our hope
of deliverance from the guilt of sin.

But in the fellowship of the cross we share
in His death and burial and resurrection, and
become partakers in His victory and righteousness. In the sixth chapter of Romans the be-

3

liever is said to be dead, buried, planted, crucified, risen, and living *with Christ.*

> " Dying together " with Jesus,
>   This is the end of strife!
> " Buried together " with Jesus,
>   This is the gate of life!
> " Quickened together " with Jesus,
>   By the touch of God's mighty breath;
> " Risen together " with Jesus,
>   Where is thy sting, O death?
>
> " Living together " with Jesus,
>   Walking this earth with God;
> Telling Him all we are doing,
>   Casting on Him every load.
> Living His life for others,
>   Seeking alone His will,
> Resting beneath His shadow,
>   With a heart ever glad and still.
>
> — *Bessie Porter.*

" If we be dead with Christ, we believe that
we shall also live with Him." Rom. 6: 8.

There is no more fatal mistake than to imagine
that we can live with Christ without having
died with Him. Let us not pass hastily by this
truth upon which hangs all our hope of living
a victorious life. It is this death with Christ
which delivers us from the power of sin, and
the consciousness of the reality of this experience gives us confidence to share also in His
life.

This fellowship with the Crucified One is not the experience of an hour or a day, but of every day and every hour. Paul says, " I am," not " I was," crucified with Christ. " Always bearing about in the body the dying of the Lord Jesus, that the life also of Jesus might be made manifest in our body." 2 Cor. 4: 10. It is this actual and continual experience of the crucifixion, that lies at the foundation of a changed life.

" God forbid that I should glory, save in the cross of our Lord Jesus Christ, by whom the world is crucified unto me, and I unto the world." Gal. 6: 14. The power of the world in Paul's life was utterly broken by his fellowship in the cross of Christ. He recognized that when the world nailed Christ to the cross, it nailed him to the cross also. Being crucified to the world, he was completely delivered from its power.

How often we see exhibited among professed Christians an apparent friendship for the world! They seem to think there is no harm in possessing and enjoying as much of the world as possible, so long as they conform to certain religious standards. They forget that " the friendship of the world is enmity with God," and that we cannot have fellowship with the crucified Christ and with the world which crucifies Him. " Whosoever therefore will be a friend of the world is the enemy of God." James 4:4. Jesus went to the cross in order to overcome the world; and His crucified, risen, and victorious life can be imparted only to those who are willing to break utterly with the world by following Him to Calvary and the tomb. On the other side of that grave the attraction of the world is broken for the one who is in fellowship with the risen Christ.

Let us consider a little more fully some of the points discussed in this chapter.

Adam was placed in this world as the father of the human race. He was its official head, and in him the whole race was represented. When he was placed on probation, the whole race was on probation; and when he fell under sin, he brought condemnation upon himself and all the human family. His nature, which had been holy, was now unholy, poisoned by the deadly disease of sin. This nature must of course be transmitted to all born into his family. So the sentence of death passed upon all men, because it was passed on this fallen Adam nature. " The only way out of any world in which we are, is by death." So the only way out of this condemned family is for a man to die himself, or in the person of the divinely appointed substitute, the Son of man.

This Adam nature that must die, Paul calls the "flesh." He says, "I know that in me (that is, in my flesh,) dwelleth no good thing." "We know that the law is spiritual: but I am carnal, sold under sin. . . . If then I do that which I would not, I consent unto the law that it is good. Now then it is no more I that do it, but sin that dwelleth in me." Rom. 7 : 18, 14-17.

He tells us that man is carnal, sold under sin; that sin dwells in him, and that no good thing dwells in him. Later he says the mind of the flesh is "enmity against God: for it is not subject to the law of God, neither indeed can be." Rom. 8 : 7.

Is it not clear, then, that this flesh, or Adam nature, is wholly and hopelessly bad, and cannot be made good? *So all the family of Adam must die, just as God said.*

But God has made a wonderful way of escape. If a member of the Adam family waits for God to inflict the inevitable and necessary penalty for sin, he is eternally lost. But if he will accept God's plan and consent to be born again,— born from above into the family of the last Adam,— he can then of his own choice consign the Adam nature to death on the cross, and as a child of the last Adam live forever.

In the light of this truth, how significant are the Saviour's words, "Verily, verily, I say unto you, Except a man be born again, he cannot see the kingdom of God." John 3:3.

It is a wonderful miracle to be born again, and no one can afford to have any uncertainty in his mind as to what it means. John Bunyan thus described the beginning of God's work in his heart:

"Upon a day the good providence of God called me to Bedford to work at my calling; and in one of the streets of that town I came to where there were three or four poor women sitting in the sun, talking about the things of God; and being now willing to hear them discourse, I drew near to hear what they said, but I heard, yet understood not; they were far above, out of my reach; for their talk was about a new birth. At this I felt my heart begin to shake, for I saw that in all my thoughts about salvation, the new birth did never enter into my mind."

So this poor man walked the streets of Bedford, asking the question asked by Nicodemus and millions of other men, "How can a man be born again?"

How many church members there are today who not only know not the power and peace of the new birth, but actually do not know how a man is born again.

We may well study with care this simple statement of the miracle of regeneration.

" In like manner you are a sinner. You cannot atone for your past sins, you cannot change your heart, and make yourself holy. But God promises to do all this for you through Christ. You *believe* that promise. You confess your sins, and give yourself to God. You *will* to serve Him. Just as surely as you do this, God will fulfil His word to you. If you believe the promise,— believe that you are forgiven and cleansed,— God supplies the fact; you are made whole, just as Christ gave the paralytic power to walk when the man believed that he was healed. It *is* so if you believe it.

" Do not wait to *feel* that you are made whole, but say, ' I believe it; it *is* so, not because I feel it, but because God has promised. . . . Through this simple act of believing God, the Holy Spirit has begotten a new life in your heart. You are as a child born into the family of God, and He loves you as He loves His Son."—*" Steps to Christ," pp. 51, 52.*

It is evident, therefore, that all those who are born into the family of Adam are under the condemnation of death. The only way of escape is to be born again into the family of Christ, the last Adam, and thus share in His life. As surely as we are born into the family of the first Adam and remain there, we are eternally lost. As surely as we are born into the family of the last Adam and remain His true children, we are eternally saved. When a man renounces sin and self, he crucifies the flesh, and is born from above. When he reckons self dead, God makes it a fact; but it is possible at any time to yield to sin, and allow the flesh to triumph. It is because he does not persistently and continuously keep on the cross, and reckon dead the old degenerate Adam nature, that he so often suffers disappointment and failure.

The only possible condition of continuous peace, joy, victory, and fellowship with God is each day, each hour, each moment, by His grace, to keep self on the cross and Christ on the throne, " bearing about in the body the dying of the Lord Jesus, that the life also of Jesus might be made manifest in our body."

THERE is an unseen battlefield
    In every human breast,
Where two opposing forces meet,
    And where they seldom rest.
That field is veiled from mortal sight,
    'Tis only seen by One
Who knows alone where victory lies
    When each day's fight is done.

— *Unknown.*

Resurrection Life

THE unbeliever is dead in trespasses and sins, but the believer, through the death and resurrection of Christ, has been made alive unto God, and shares His divine life, energy, and ability to triumph over sin.

Paul says in Romans 6 : 5, " If we have been planted together in the likeness of His death, we shall be also in the likeness of His resurrection."

As it means much to the believer to share in Christ's death, it means much also to share in His resurrection. " Like as Christ was raised up from the dead by the glory of the Father, even so we also should walk in newness of life." Rom. 6 : 4.

Among all the miracles and proofs of Christ's divinity, perhaps the crowning one was His own resurrection. In it was manifest the glory of the Father. The Saviour's mighty works of restoring sight to the blind, hearing to the deaf, speech to the dumb, and life to the dead, were all included in the miracle of His own resurrection. He hung on the cross until He " gave up the ghost." His heart was pierced by the Roman spear, and He was wrapped in embalming cloths and laid in the tomb. What a stupendous miracle when He awoke, arose, and came forth from the grave, "declared to be the Son of God with power, according to the spirit of holiness, by the resurrection from the dead." Rom. 1: 4.

Henceforth believers are to look upon this miracle as the unit of measurement of God's power to deliver His people. How many times in past generations had Israel heard the words, "I am the Lord thy God, which brought thee out of the land of Egypt." Ps. 81: 10. Their deliverance from the destroying angel, their protection under the canopy of the fiery cloud, their victory in the overthrow of their enemies in the sea, all these miracles attested the power of the One who was pledged to bring them into the Land of Promise triumphant over all their foes.

But now, when struggling with strong temptation and buffeted by the enemy, we are bidden to trust in the One who raised Christ from the dead. Were we dependent upon our own efforts and struggles to overcome, we might well give up the conflict in despair. But who can doubt the sufficiency of divine grace as measured by the "exceeding greatness of His power to usward who believe, according to the working of His mighty power, which He wrought in Christ, when He raised Him from the dead, and set Him

at His own right hand in the heavenly places."
Eph. 1 : 19, 20.

And we are to share in the " likeness of His
resurrection." " Knowing this, that our old
man is crucified with Him, that the body of sin
might be destroyed, that henceforth we should
not serve sin. For he that is dead is freed from
sin. Now if we be dead with Christ, we believe
that we shall also live with Him." Rom. 6 : 6-8.

Christ went into the grave, slain by sin. He
came forth an eternal victor, and those who
come forth with Him are henceforth freed from
the power and dominion of sin. They regard
Christ's death as their death, Christ's grave as
their grave, Christ's resurrection as their resurrection, and Christ's victory as their victory.
They are to remember that " Christ being raised
from the dead dieth no more; death hath no
more dominion over Him." Verse 9. And since
He can no more be brought under the dominion
of death, which is the dominion of sin, those
who share with Him this resurrection life also
share this victory over sin and over the second
death.

We may well ponder the statement of Andrew
Murray, " The believer is to remember that the
roots of his being are in Christ's grave. The
oak stands in the grave of the acorn from which
it sprang, and to remove it is to destroy it.

However massive the tree, it never loses its connection with that buried seed."

Christ said, " Except a corn of wheat fall into the ground and die, it abideth alone: but if it die, it bringeth forth much fruit. He that loveth his life shall lose it; and he that hateth his life in this world shall keep it unto life eternal." John 12: 24, 25. Through His own death, burial, and resurrection, Christ brought many sons into glory, and every true believer dies and is buried, not to remain in the grave, but to come forth with a new life of power and fruitfulness.

Consider the actual humanity of Jesus before His death. He was as truly a man as any child of Adam. He declared, " I can of Mine own self do nothing." John 5: 30. As the Son of man, He was bound by the weakness of humanity and oppressed by sin. His miracles were wrought through Him by the Holy Spirit, as they have been through other men who were yielded to God. While actually the Son of God, He clothed His divinity with humanity, and in that human personality was as dependent upon the Father as any one of His human brothers.

But after His death and resurrection, all this was changed. No longer was divinity clothed with humanity, but humanity was clothed with divinity. Having ascended to heaven and received the Father's approval of His whole life and sacrifice, He declared: "All power is given unto Me in heaven and in earth." Matt. 28 : 18 This is the resurrection life.

Christ came forth from the grave — still the Son of man, but conqueror of the grave and victor over sin, not only for Himself, but for His brother men.

As the carpenter of Nazareth, and the teacher of Israel, He lived a life of toil and care, of many sorrows and fierce temptations and conflicts with the enemy, of physical weariness and pain, of long night vigils, of prayers and tears and supplications for strength to do the Father's will.

The victory which He thus wrought out He imparts to His children today. From the grave He came forth as a king, a mighty conqueror, with the keys of death and hell in his hand, having gained the victory over all the power of the enemy.

When we share in His life, let us remember that it is this resurrection life. It is a life that has already triumphed *in human nature* over all sin, all temptation, the world, the flesh, and the devil, death and the grave. "If we have been planted together in the likeness of His death, we shall be also in the likeness of His resurrection." Rom. 6 : 5.

As we enter through faith into His death, burial, and resurrection experience, we share in His victory. "For by the death which He died He became, once for all, dead in relation to sin; but by the life which he now lives *He is alive in relation to God.* In the same way you also must regard yourselves as dead in relation to sin, *but as alive in relation to God, because you are in Christ Jesus.*" Rom. 6:10, 11 (Weymouth).

Peace, Perfect Peace

PEACE, perfect peace, in this dark world of sin!
The blood of Jesus whispers peace within.

Peace, perfect peace, with thronging duties pressed!
To do the will of Jesus, this is rest.

Peace, perfect peace, with sorrow surging round!
On Jesus' bosom naught but calm is found.

Peace, perfect peace, with loved ones far away!
In Jesus' keeping we are safe, and they.

Peace, perfect peace, our future here unknown!
Jesus we know, and He is on the throne.

Peace, perfect peace, death shadowing us and ours!
Jesus has vanquished death and all its powers.

It is enough; earth's struggles soon will cease.
And Jesus' call to heaven's perfect peace.

— *Bickersteth.*

Faith Makes It So

" IF we be dead with Christ, we believe that we shall also live with Him. . . . For in that He died, He died unto sin once: but in that He liveth, He liveth unto God." Rom. 6: 8-10.

How significant are the statements in these two verses! He died to sin. We died with Him. He liveth unto God. We shall also live with Him.

There can be no question as to what is meant by the believer's dying with Christ. It is a death to sin. It breaks all ties between him and the sins which have enslaved him. He is to regard his connection with sin severed as completely as that of the silent form lying in the casket ready for the tomb.

The new life is to be lived wholly unto God. It is not his own. It is " bought with a price," even the precious blood of Christ. But we must remember that only as this life is wholly of God can it be lived wholly to God. It is not found in struggle or self-effort, nor in culture, education, or religious ceremonies; but is the gift of God imparted by His Spirit in response to faith. It is as much a miracle as the restoration of sight to the blind, hearing to the deaf, or life

63

to the dead. It is hard for those who are slaves to sin and evil habits they have long sought to overcome, to believe that by simply accepting Christ and yielding to Him they instantly receive a new nature, and power enabling them to live a new life. Yet this is true, and count-less thousands have experienced this mighty miracle.

In our study of Romans 6 we come to a state-ment which is like the keystone to an arch. This is the point where the connection is made between the divine plan and the believer's experience. In this, as in all other cases, the connection is made by faith. "Likewise reckon ye also yourselves to be dead indeed unto sin, but alive unto God through Jesus Christ our Lord." Verse 11.

The moment a sinner becomes united to Christ by faith, God regards him as judicially dead to sin. Now He tells us that it is the believer's duty to join with God in reckoning himself dead to sin, and then, by the power of the Holy Spirit within, this judicial death is experienced.

Every man must accept God's provision for his death to sin, and must reckon it so, before he is actually dead to sin by experience. He must reckon himself dead to sin first by faith, and then God makes that faith a reality.

It is exactly the same manner· in which pardon for sin becomes experimental. The sinner confesses and asks forgiveness, but if he does not believe God pardons, he is not forgiven. If he *does* believe, he *is* forgiven.

" You confess your sins and give yourself to God. You *will* to serve Him. Just as surely as you do this, God will fulfil His word to you. If you believe the promise,— believe that you are forgiven and cleansed,— God supplies the fact; you are made whole, just as Christ gave the paralytic power to walk when the man believed that he was healed. It *is* so if you believe it." —" *Steps to Christ*," *p. 51.*

In the same manner it is necessary to reckon ourselves dead to sin before God can make it a fact in our personal experience. And it is evident that no man will be dead indeed unto sin until he obeys God and claims this death by faith.

It is said that for weeks after the proclamation was issued emancipating the slaves in the South, many Negroes in remote places went on toiling as before. They did not know they had been legally freed, and therefore had no knowledge or hope of experimental freedom. But even after some heard the truth, they did not believe it, and went on as before. Though legally free, they were still experimentally in slavery, because of unbelief in the provision made for their liberty.

How many of Christ's followers are like those poor slaves — still in bondage and slavery to sin because they refuse to " reckon " themselves " dead indeed unto sin " through the death of Jesus Christ.

Having entered this experience by faith, there is a solemn warning against continuing in sin: " Neither yield ye your members as instruments of unrighteousness unto sin." Rom. 6 : 13.

" Know ye not, that to whom ye yield yourselves servants to obey, his servants ye are to whom ye obey; whether of sin unto death, or of obedience unto righteousness ? " Verse 16.

The believer must " reckon " himself " dead indeed unto sin," and then " sin shall not have dominion " over him. But if he now yields his members to unrighteousness, it is sin, and sin is unto death. " For the end of those things is death." " The wages of sin is death." Rom. 6 : 14, 21, 23.

These statements are given to the believer, the child of God. If he persists in indulging the appetites of the flesh, reverting to the old life and yielding to its evil habits, in the end this indulgence will neutralize all the power of the gospel, and " sin leads to death, ends in death, and is paid its wages in death."

Some, appropriating the precious promises of God with simple, childlike faith, enter at once into a new and fuller life. A few words from a recent letter from one earnestly seeking this life, illustrate the point:

" The evening after I arrived home I chanced upon a very appropriate text. Without thinking where I was about to read, I opened at the first chapter of Colossians, and my eye fell on the thirteenth verse, ' Who *hath* delivered us from the *power* of darkness.' That was a real message to me. Then I began farther up, and read the eleventh verse, ' Strengthened with *all* might, according to His glorious power, unto *all* patience and long-suffering *with joyfulness.*' I took that for my goal."

There may be those who question about the word " reckon," and ask, " How can I reckon I am dead to sin when I know that I am not ? " To them it seems like a mere exercise of the imagination. But such miss the real thought back of this word, which simply calls for the exercise of practical faith. No man ever knows whether he is forgiven except as he takes God at His word. He reckons himself pardoned because that is what God promises. The moment he meets the conditions and reckons himself pardoned, it is done. It is no more difficult to reckon himself dead to sin when God says he is dead, than to reckon his sins forgiven according to God's promise.

If we transfer our hope from human struggle to the promises of God, the only limit to our attainment is that of our own faith.

This is illustrated by the experience of Peter. Jesus appeared, walking on the water. It was evidently some distance, for the Saviour was seen too dimly to be recognized with certainty. When He was finally recognized, Peter joyfully cried, "Lord, if it be Thou, bid me come unto Thee on the water. And He said, Come."

Springing out of the boat, Peter walked upon the water nearly the whole distance with his eyes fixed upon Jesus. But when almost at His Master's side he looked away, was frightened by the wind and waves, and began to sink. Peter had done what was otherwise impossible, because he was in touch with Christ by faith. The instant that touch was broken, the power was gone. One moment he was strong to do the impossible, the next he was helpless and sinking.

So in the matter of living unto God — the victorious life — it is a miracle as truly as walking on the water. One moment a man may be strong to overcome all the powers of evil arrayed against him; the next he may sink in sin. It all depends upon the vital connection of faith by which his unity with Christ is maintained.

The moment we lay hold upon any promise of God by faith, having met the conditions, the blessing is ours. It is so if we believe it. Again and again the Scriptures illustrate most emphatically how salvation is complete in Christ and may be secured only by faith.

"By grace are ye saved through faith; and that not of yourselves: it is the gift of God: not of works, lest any man should boast." Eph. 2:8, 9.

There is an old story of a Chinese Christian who was telling a heathen friend the difference between the Christian religion and heathen religions. He said:

"One day a man fell into a deep well. He could not possibly climb out. No one could hear his cries for help. After frantic struggles he gave up in despair. Then Buddha appeared, and looking down in the well, said, 'If you will come up here, I will teach you so that you will not fall into another well.' But the poor man could not climb out. Next came Confucius, who said, 'You poor man, had you obeyed my teachings, you would not have fallen into this well.' And again he was left to perish. Then Jesus came, and seeing his lost condition, Himself sprang into the well, and lifted the man out."

This is strikingly like the experience of David. He says in Psalms 40:1-3:

" I waited patiently for the Lord; and He inclined unto me, and heard my cry. He brought me up also out of an horrible pit, out of the miry clay, and set my feet upon a rock, and established my goings. And He hath put a new song in my mouth, even praise unto our God: many shall see it, and fear, and shall trust in the Lord." Ps. 40: 1-3.

It is important to notice what David did:

" I waited patiently."

And then what the Lord did:

" He inclined unto me, and heard my cry."

" He brought me up also out of an horrible pit."

He " set my feet upon a rock."

He " established my goings."

He " put a new song in my mouth."

Could any illustration be found to teach more absolutely that salvation in Christ is a finished work? He does not help us to climb out of the pit of sin. He lifts us out. He does not leave us on slippery ground, but sets our feet upon a rock. He does not leave us weak and helpless to fall from the rock, but He establishes our goings. And then He puts a song of praise in our mouth that charms and captivates other lost ones, and wins them to the Saviour.

Blessed be His name, He saves " to the uttermost " all who come unto God by Him, " seeing He ever liveth to make intercession for them."

Right Action of the Will

IN Romans 13:14 Paul says, "Put ye on the Lord Jesus Christ, and make not provision for the flesh, to fulfil the lusts thereof." This is the practical equivalent of Romans 6:11: "Likewise reckon ye also yourselves to be dead indeed unto sin, but alive unto God through Jesus Christ our Lord." But this reckoning must be more than the exercise of the imagination or a mere passive consent to what God says. Faith is an active principle, a mighty force, and this judicial freedom provided by God must be laid hold of by faith that comes from God and has in it the energy of God. There is no virtue whatever in saying, "I reckon myself dead to my violent temper, but of course I expect I shall get angry sometimes."

To count on sinning is a form of unbelief, and that is sin. We make provision for many things day by day, planning for our clothing, our food, and other temporal wants. But if a man knew that he would die today, he would not plan longer for living, but would immediately cease preparation for living and prepare for dying. God proposes that our union with Christ shall make death to sin a great reality in our lives, so that we shall reckon ourselves dead to sin, immediately cease all provision for sinning, and plan only to live the new life in Christ Jesus.

This reckoning of death to sin and expectation of triumph over sin has a profound effect upon the life. One who expects to sin will sin, but one who reckons himself no longer under sin's dominion, but victorious through the indwelling Christ, is fortified by his very attitude, and actually challenges God to make good that deliverance upon which His child confidently relies. The fact that he trusts humbly and implicitly in the promises, makes it certain that God will fulfil them to the uttermost. " The secret of true and full holiness is by faith and in the power of the Holy Spirit to live in the consciousness, I am dead to sin."

" Let not sin therefore reign in your mortal body, that ye should obey it in the lusts thereof. Neither yield ye your members as instruments of unrighteousness unto sin: but yield yourselves unto God, *as those that are alive from the dead,* and your members as instruments of righteousness unto God. For sin shall not have dominion over you: for ye are not under the law, but under grace." Rom. 6 : 12, 13.

In the previous chapter the emphasis is on the word " reckon." In this it is on the word " yield." First, " yield " not your members " as instruments of unrighteousness; " second, " yield yourselves unto God."

The great decisive factor in the life is the will. Sin has its roots in the will, and through the will holds the sinner in slavery. But when the will is exercised in renouncing sin and choosing Christ as master, the same power which changes the heart and imparts a new life, also changes the will. The unbeliever willed only to please self. Now he wills to please and obey God. But he remains a free moral agent. True obedience to God is never compulsory, but remains forever voluntary and prompted by love.

Hence it is still possible for the believer to yield to those tendencies to sin which have become habitual to the body.

It is clearly implied in the text that the way of victory over these temptations is not to struggle, but to yield in faith to the new Master. No man can have two masters; and an active, conscious yielding to Christ leaves no room for the dominance of the old master whom we have renounced forever. By withholding our members from him and yielding them to God, we enable God to make actual and experimental what He already reckons us to be as His children.

We are at first declared justified, judicially freed from the condemnation of the law; but now, being born into the family of God as sons,

4

we must demonstrate this relationship by a holy
life. What a dishonor to God to have children
who are yet the slaves of sin! It would testify
either that God was unable to rescue His own
children from the enemy, or that sin is more
attractive to His children than holiness. " Yield
yourselves unto God, as those that are alive
from the dead." Rom. 6 : 13. Not until his
death with Christ to sin and his burial have become a great reality, can the believer appreciate
and understand the new life. The only life
Jesus has now to impart is His resurrected life.
It is the life the other side of the infliction of
the death penalty for sin. If we have died with
Him, and yet live, truly the life we now live is
His life. We can live this life only " by the faith
of the Son of God," who loved us and gave Himself for us. Gal. 2 : 20.

" We are not under the law, but under grace."
Rom. 6 : 15. The law places before us a standard, and demands obedience, but it imparts no
power to obey. It says, " Do and live." It requires, but does not enable.

Grace holds before us the same divine standard, and then offers power to meet the requirements. It says, " Believe and accept." The
strength, the obedience, the righteousness, are
all of God through faith. Grace does not set
aside the law which is God's standard of right-

eousness. But of one who is not under the law but under grace Paul says, "It is God which worketh in you both to will and to do of His good pleasure." Phil. 2:13.

It may be wise to discuss here more fully the immense importance of yielding the will and making a complete and continuous surrender to God.

"The Christian life is a battle and a march. But the victory to be gained is not won by human power. The field of conflict is the domain of the heart. The battle which we have to fight — the greatest battle that was ever fought by man — is the surrender of self to the will of God, the yielding of the heart to the sovereignty of love. The old nature, born of blood and of the will of the flesh, cannot inherit the kingdom of God. . . .

"He who determines to enter the spiritual kingdom will find that all the powers and passions of an unregenerate nature, backed by the forces of the kingdom of darkness, are arrayed against him."—"The Mount of Blessing," pp. 203, 204.

Though opposed by forces within and without, the power to surrender the will and open the heart to God is possessed by every human being. "The power of choice God has given to men; it is theirs to exercise. You cannot change your heart; you cannot of yourself give to God its affections; but you can *choose* to serve Him. You can give Him your will; He will then work in you to will and to do according to His good pleasure."—*" Steps to Christ,"* p. 47.

Those who fight this great battle to the point of real surrender, enter a new world in the Christian experience, as the following extract from a letter witnesses:

" That motto, ' Let go, and let God,' appealed to me as such a good one. I cannot remember that I ever heard it before. It kept ringing in my ears, and as I left the college that last night, I determined to go home and settle the matter before going to sleep. The folks had retired, so I sat down by the fire and thought it over. Then I prayed something like this: ' Dear Lord, *I will* let go — as far as lies within my power, I will let go. Let come what may, only sustain me by Thy grace. Dear Lord, I do let go of it all.' And I surrendered — I let go, then and there.

" That prayer the Lord heard and answered without any delay. Immediately the burden was lifted and the light came. My soul was filled with peace and joy and a blessed relief that I never before had experienced to such an extent. I was abundantly blessed beyond anything I had ever thought of. I have never seen the Christian life in its beauty, simplicity, and reality as I do

RIGHT ACTION OF THE WILL

now. There is a fuller, richer, deeper meaning in the promises of God.

"What an unwise thing to make the least vestige of reserve! I have learned that God does not accept service, time, money, or anything else as a substitute for a fully surrendered heart and will."

This surrender should be made once for all, and then repeated every day and made a continuous experience.

"Through the right exercise of the will, an entire change may be made in your life. By yielding up your will to Christ, you ally yourself with the power that is above all principalities and powers. You will have strength from above to hold you steadfast, and thus through *constant* surrender to God you will be enabled to live the new life, even the life of faith."— "*Steps to Christ*," *p. 48.*

As this surrender is maintained day by day, the way grows brighter and more delightful because of fellowship with Christ.

"By His perfect obedience He has made it possible for every human being to obey God's commandments. When we submit ourselves to Christ, the heart is united with His heart, the will is merged in His will, the mind becomes one with His mind, the thoughts are brought into captivity to Him; we live His life. This is what it means to be clothed with the garment of His righteousness."—"*Christ's Object Lessons,*" *page 312.*

Wounded Nursing the Wounded

WHEN, wounded sore, the stricken soul
    Lies bleeding and unbound,
One only hand, a piercèd hand,
    Can heal the sinner's wound.

When sorrow swells the laden breast,
    And tears of anguish flow,
One only heart, a broken heart,
    Can feel the sinner's woe.

When penitence has wept in vain
    Over some foul, dark spot,
One only stream, a stream of blood,
    Can wash away the blot.

'Tis Jesus' blood that washes white,
    His hand that brings relief,
His heart that's touched with all our joys,
    And feels for all our grief.

Lift up Thy bleeding hand, O Lord,
    Unseal that cleansing tide;
We have no shelter from our sin
    But in Thy wounded side.

              — *Mrs. C. F. Alexander.*

The Closest Union

THE seventh chapter of Romans opens with a new and striking illustration, which presents a different aspect of the doctrine of our union with Christ:

" The woman which hath an husband is bound by the law to her husband so long as he liveth; but if the husband be dead, she is loosed from the law of her husband. So then if, while her husband liveth, she be married to another man, she shall be called an adulteress: but if her husband be dead, she is free from that law; so that she is no adulteress, though she be married to another man."

Here the sinner is represented as a woman bound to her husband by the law of marriage. The husband represents the flesh, or " old man." As the woman is bound to her husband as long as he lives, so the sinner is bound to his natural sinful flesh, and can be released only by death. So long as the old man of sin lives, all his profession of religion is hypocrisy, or spiritual adultery. " But if the husband be dead, she is loosed from the law of her husband."

" Wherefore, my brethren, ye also are become dead to the law by the body of Christ." It is in the body of Christ crucified that our " old man" dies, and we are delivered from the condemnation of the law, and free to enter that closest, most sacred relationship with Him.

"When we were in the flesh, the motions of sin, which were by the law, did work in our members to bring forth fruit unto death." So long as the " old man " lived, the motions, or passions, of sins which are condemned by the law were constantly bringing forth fruit unto death. We were helpless in the grasp of those evil tendencies and lusts which characterized the " old man," and which kept us continually under condemnation of the law. " But now we are delivered from the law, that being dead wherein we were held." " Knowing this, that our old man is crucified with Him, that the body of sin might be destroyed, that henceforth we should not serve sin." Rom. 6: 6.

What an impressive figure is here presented! A woman is bound to a degraded husband who subjects her to every cruel bondage and indignity. She cannot marry another, but is bound to him so long as he lives. But when the husband dies, he has no further claim upon her. She is free to marry another.

What blessed assurance this brings to one who recognizes the loathsome nature of sin, and longs for deliverance from the flesh! That freedom does not come by compromise or separation or abandonment, but by death, even our death with Christ. In Christ our "old man" is crucified, dead, and buried. And "now we are delivered from the law, that being dead wherein we were held," "that ye should be married to another, even to Him who is raised from the dead."

Here is presented one of the most beautiful and significant figures by which the believer's union with Christ is illustrated. In the legal union of Romans 6 his identity with Christ is represented by his relation to the last Adam as head of the race. Here it is the identity of husband and wife, the closest and holiest union of which we know.

The wife leaves father and mother, and cleaves to her husband. She gives up her family and name. Her means and her own life she surrenders to him, to become henceforth dependent upon his loving will and care. And they two become one flesh.

More than this, the two lives thus merged into one become the source of life, and this is used as a figure of the holy fruitfulness of the true believer. "That ye should be married to another, even to Him who is raised from the dead, that we should bring forth fruit unto God." How futile all spectacular services and ostentatious activities, and how displeasing they must be to God when offered as a substitute for that holy devotion of wife to husband which seeks only to please and exalt the object of supreme affection! How little believers appreciate the exalted blessing and privilege of their relationship with Christ!

All the boundless resources of the divine Bridegroom are for the exaltation and satisfaction of the bride. On the other hand, some of the most solemn warnings given in the Scripture concern the peril of treating lightly this sacred relation. To enter this union with Christ and then give Him anything but the supreme place in the heart, is spiritual adultery. "Ye adulterers and adulteresses, know ye not that the friendship of the world is enmity with God? whosoever therefore will be a friend of the world is the enemy of God." James 4:4.

The believer regards himself as the bride of Christ, but he must not forget that if he trifles with sin and tolerates in his life those things that pertain to the world, his course will as surely destroy this union as adultery will destroy the sacred ties of marriage. It is like the daring of the wife who, while enjoying the privileges and comforts provided by her husband's love and the protection and honor of his name, by flirting and coquetry maintains a dishonorable intimacy with other men. What must

be the real condition of the believer who seems
continually fascinated with the glamour and
tinsel of the world, and inquires how far he
can go in its follies and pleasures and still be
permitted to retain his name on the church
records? Such an attitude is evidence of a
selfish, formal profession, which knows little of
the vital union with Christ described in Romans
6, and still less of that loyal devotion to Christ
and satisfaction in Him which the true bride
feels for the bridegroom who has won her heart.

"So near, so very near to God, I cannot nearer be,
For, in the person of His Son, I am as near as He.
So dear, so very dear to God, I cannot dearer be,
For, in the person of his Son, I am as dear as He."

Love's Argument

I BORE with thee long, weary days and nights,
　Through many pangs of heart, through many tears.
I bore with thee, thy hardness, coldness, slights,
　For three and thirty years.

Who else had dared for thee what I have dared?
　I plunged the depth most deep from bliss above;
I not My flesh, I not My spirit, spared;
　Give thou Me love for love!

For thee I thirsted in the daily drouth,
　For thee I trembled in the nightly frost.
Much sweeter thou than honey to My mouth;
　Why wilt thou still be lost?

I bore thee on My shoulders, and rejoiced.
　Men only marked upon My shoulders borne
The branding cross, and shouted, hungry-voiced,
　Or wagged their heads in scorn.

Thee did nails grave upon My hands. Thy name
　Did thorns for frontlets stamp between My eyes.
I, Holy One, put on thy guilt and shame;
　I, God, Priest, Sacrifice.

A thief upon My right hand and My left,
　Six hours alone, athirst, in misery;
At length in death one smote My heart, and cleft
　A hiding place for thee.

Nailed to the racking cross, than bed of down
　More dear, whereon to stretch Myself and sleep,
So did I win a kingdom — share My crown!
　A harvest — come and reap!

　　　　　　　　　　— *Christina Rosetti.*

The Power Provided

ACCORDING to the figure first introduced in Romans 7, he to whom we were formerly married — the flesh, or old man — is reckoned dead, and we are now married to another, "even to Him who is raised from the dead."

That this relationship results in intense sensitiveness to sin, is the thought next introduced in verses 7-24. What a vivid description is this of the experience through which we all pass when sin grows more and more hideous and hateful because we are drawing nearer to the One who is perfect purity, holiness, and divine excellence of character.

"The closer you come to Jesus, the more faulty you will appear in your own eyes; for your vision will be clearer, and your imperfections will be seen in broad and distinct contrast to His perfect nature. . . . No deep-seated love for Jesus can dwell in the heart that does not realize its own sinfulness.

"The soul that is transformed by the grace of Christ will admire His divine character; but if we do not see our own moral deformity, it is unmistakable evidence that we have not had a

view of the beauty and excellence of Christ."
—"*Steps to Christ*," *pp. 64, 65.*

As we see our own hearts, deceitful and desperately wicked, we long for complete deliverance and victory, and with sincere resolutions and firm determination we begin the struggle to attain it. Again and again our fight seems to end in ignominious failure and defeat, until in despair we cry, " O wretched man that I am! who shall deliver me from the body of this death? " And this seems the opportune time for the revelation to the soul of that light which makes the way clear for the realization of its goal.

Up to this point in Paul's argument for not continuing in sin, the agency of the Holy Spirit has not been mentioned. In fact, no reference is made to the Spirit thus far in the epistle, except in the fourth verse of the first chapter and the fifth verse of the fifth chapter.

He has dealt with the awful fall and ruin wrought by sin, the working of the law, the crucifixion, burial, and resurrection of Christ, and our identification with Him in this experience by faith, bringing justification and life through His death. This is followed by legal deliverance from the dominion of sin and the condemnation of the law, full surrender to Christ and union with Him in spiritual wedlock, in order that we may bring forth fruit unto God.

Though understanding these great facts and truths, the believer is conscious of his inability to escape the awful power of habitual sin. He is confident that there is a way by which all these precious truths may become actual experiences, but that way of deliverance has not yet been made clear.

Now the link which completes the chain of testimony in his emancipation is supplied. It is the Spirit who has convicted of sin and the Spirit who has revealed Christ; but now there comes a revelation of the Spirit Himself as a living, indwelling, divine Presence, entering with all the fulness of omnipotent power to make real in Paul the divine plan; and he shouts in triumph and gratitude, " I thank God through Jesus Christ our Lord."

Forty-eight times in chapter 7 : 7-25 occur the personal pronouns *I, me,* and *my.* The knowledge and desires and ideals are right, but there is no power in human resolutions to reach the standard. The office of the Holy Spirit has not been recognized. All that the believer has learned of the blessed provisions for full salvation in the first seven chapters are only facts and theories until made experience by the Holy Spirit. Through His mighty power the image of Jesus Christ is reproduced in the believer's soul.

"We all, with open face beholding as in a glass the glory of the Lord, are changed into the same image from glory to glory, even as by the Spirit of the Lord." 2 Cor. 3:18.

It is this gracious work of the Spirit that is so fully discussed in Romans 8, there being at least seventeen statements describing the Holy Spirit's relation to, and operation within, the believer.

"There is therefore now no condemnation to them which are in Christ Jesus, who walk not after the flesh, but after the Spirit. For the law of the Spirit of life in Christ Jesus hath made me free from the law of sin and death. For what the law could not do, in that it was weak through the flesh, God sending His own Son in the likeness of sinful flesh, and for sin, condemned sin in the flesh: that the righteousness of the law might be fulfilled in us who walk not after the flesh, but after the Spirit." Rom. 8:1-4.

Here is no longer conflict and struggle, disappointment, defeat, and discouragement; but through the mighty power of the Spirit alone, justification has come in place of condemnation, life in place of death, freedom in place of bondage, strength in place of weakness, obedience in place of transgression, success in place of failure. And this is all the result of being " in Christ " through the ministry of the Holy Spirit.

" They that are after the flesh do mind the things of the flesh; but they that are after the Spirit the things of the Spirit. For to be carnally minded is death; but' to be spiritually minded is life and peace. Because the carnal mind is enmity against God: for it is not subject to the law of God, neither indeed can be. So then they that are in the flesh cannot please God." Verses 5-8.

With our natural human limitations and lack of wisdom and understanding of divine things, we do not see how we can live up to our high standing as sons of God. But the Spirit graciously makes up for all our ignorance and deficiencies, prompting us to prayer, and making intercession for us with superhuman energy.

How adequate and complete is the help here attributed to the working of the Holy Spirit in behalf of the believer. He delivers from all condemnation, frees from the law of sin and death, imparts strength, righteousness, a renewed mind, a Christlike spirit. He quickens the body, subdues its sinful tendencies and appetites, lets in the light, and imparts assurance, consciousness of sonship and heirship, help for our infirmities, and divine assistance in prayer.

It is clear that this wonderful revelation of the Spirit's ministry explains the twenty-fourth and twenty-fifth verses of chapter 7. After the awful struggle, characterized by deep conviction and intense longing and striving for holiness, which ends only in disappointment, Paul cries, "O wretched man that I am! who shall deliver me from the body of this death?" And then with the revelation of the Spirit's mighty agency, more than adequate for all his needs, he utters the triumphant shout, "I thank God through Jesus Christ our Lord."

"The Spirit was to be given as a regenerating agent, and without this the sacrifice of Christ would have been of no avail. . . . Sin could be resisted and overcome only through the mighty agency of the third person of the Godhead, who would come with no modified energy, but in the fulness of divine power. It is the Spirit that makes effectual what has been wrought out by the world's Redeemer. It is by the Spirit that the heart is made pure. Through the Spirit the believer becomes a partaker of the divine nature.

"Christ has given His Spirit as a divine power to overcome all hereditary and cultivated tendencies to evil, and to impress His own character upon His church."—"*The Desire of Ages,*" *page 671.*

It is through Jesus Christ, because by virtue of His merits and ministry the Holy Spirit came down upon the church at Pentecost as His representative and successor. Through the death and shed blood of Christ we are justified; through the agency of the Spirit sent forth from heaven by the ministry of our Lord, we are sanctified. We could never be justified without His death and resurrection, nor could we be sanctified without His life and intercession resulting in the descent of the Spirit upon the church, and upon each individual believer. Every child of God becomes a temple of the Holy Ghost. As he yields without reserve to be filled, possessed, controlled, and led by the Spirit, every hereditary and cultivated tendency to sin is subdued, and he receives divine life, liberty, power, and victory.

Poor, sad humanity,
Through all the dust and heat,
Turns back, with bleeding feet,
By the weary road it came,
Unto the simple thought
By the Great Master taught,
And that remaineth still:
Not he that repeateth the name,
But he that doeth the will!
— *Longfellow's " St. John."*

Transverse or Parallel

DEAR LORD, my will from Thine doth run
   Too oft a different way;
I cannot say, " Thy will be done,"
   In every darkened day;
     My heart grows chill
     To see Thy will
   Turn all earth's gold to gray.

My will is set to gather flowers,
   Thine blights them in my hand;
Mine reaches for life's sunny hours,
   Thine leads through shadow-land.
     And all my days
     Go on in ways
   I cannot understand.

Yet more and more this truth doth shine
   From failure and from loss:
The will that runs transverse to Thine,
   Doth thereby make it cross;
     Thine upright will
     Cuts straight and still
   Through pride and dream and dross.

But if in parallel to Thine
   My will doth meekly run,
All things in heaven and earth are mine;
   My will is crossed by none,—
     Thou art in me,
     And I in Thee —
   Thy will and mine are done.
                — *Bishop Huntington.*

The Laws of Death and Life

THE climax of the experience of conscious failure and defeat in Romans 7 is reached in the words: " O wretched man that I am! who shall deliver me from the body of this death? "

As the eighth chapter describes a wholly opposite experience of conscious and continuous victory, its climax is in striking contrast, " Nay, in all these things we are more than conquerors through Him that loved us." Rom. 8:37.

It is one thing to conquer after a long and fierce conflict by merely averting defeat. It is another thing to be more than conqueror — to know that at no moment is there any question of ultimate and complete victory; to push the battle into the enemy's territory, and drive him before us a defeated and impotent foe. This is being more than conqueror, and this is ours through Him that loved us. So far as we are concerned, it is a victory of love — love that lifts us out of the element of sin and failure and defeat into the atmosphere of His own life. This is all a matter of spiritual law. In the seventh chapter, the testimony is:

"I find then a law, that, when I would do good, evil is present with me. For I delight in the law of God after the inward man; but I see another law in my members, warring against the law of my mind, and bringing me into captivity to the law of sin." Rom. 7: 21-23.

Now what has become of this law in the eighth chapter? Has it been removed or destroyed, so that there is no more temptation or tendency to sin, as so many seem to expect? No more than the natural law that prevents a man's living under water is done away when he descends in the diving apparatus. The law or tendency remains, but it is completely overcome or counteracted by the higher law which provides the means of life from above.

So Paul says: "The law of the Spirit of life in Christ Jesus hath made me free from the law of sin and death." Rom. 8: 2.

It is this working of the law of the Spirit of life that continually counteracts the law of sin and death, and makes it possible for the life of Christ's disciples to be "like His, a series of uninterrupted victories." God's child is not a slave fighting to obtain his freedom, but a free man fighting to maintain the liberty secured to him in Christ. Freedom is not the goal to be won as the result of the Christian warfare, but is the necessary condition of a victorious life.

This is made very plain by one of Evan Hopkins' vivid illustrations:

The natural law of a room at night is to be dark. This tendency is not destroyed by bringing in a lighted lamp, but it is completely counteracted so long as the lighted lamp remains. If it is removed, the tendency is again evident, for darkness reigns.

The dark room represents our hearts, and the tendency to darkness represents the law of sin working in our members. The lamp is Christ. On His entering our hearts, the tendency and possibility to sin are not destroyed, but His presence completely counteracts the working of the law of sin, so long as He reigns within. Thus the law of the Spirit of life in Christ Jesus makes me free from the law of sin and death. And by this blessed ministry of the Spirit we are more than conquerors through Him that loved us.

But many are perplexed concerning this experience, because, though they are certain of a very real victory in Christ, their victory is not complete. It seems to be partial or fragmentary, and they long to be "all Christ's all the time."

Our experience seems to teach that we are more like a house with many rooms, than like one room. We may invite the Spirit to come in and make Christ real within. We may fully

surrender the best room to Him, and we may
yield up another room, and still another, to be
occupied and possessed by the divine Guest. Bu
the fulness of His blessing can come only when
the last room is surrendered, and He is crowned
King of all, while we withdraw and leave Him
in undisputed control of the utmost limit of our
being.

Many talk of getting more of the Holy Spirit,
but what we all need is to let the Holy Spirit
have more of us until the remotest corner of
every room is filled with His presence. This is
the blessed life of victory, the new life in Christ
Jesus. It is the life that means inseparable
union with Him.

"I am persuaded, that neither death, nor life,
nor angels, nor principalities, nor powers, nor
things present, nor things to come, nor height,
nor depth, nor any other creature, shall be able
to separate us from the love of God, which is in
Christ Jesus our Lord." Rom. 8: 38, 39.

In Christ

IN the first verse of Romans 8 Paul says, " There is therefore now no condemnation to them which are *in Christ Jesus.*" In the tenth verse: " If *Christ be in you, the body* is dead because of sin."

Here is a striking paradox, very similar to that given by the Saviour in His beautiful lesson on the true vine, " Abide in Me, and I in you." John 15:4.

In writing to the Colossians of his call to the ministry, Paul speaks of his divine commission to proclaim the glorious mystery of the gospel to the Gentiles. This mystery, now made plain to the saints, he sums up in the expression, " Christ in you." Col. 1:27. This was not an expression of mere abstract theory, but of his own personal experience, for he wrote to the Galatians: " I am crucified with Christ: nevertheless I live; yet not I, but *Christ liveth in me.*" Gal. 2:20.

And so we have the stirring exhortation to the Corinthians: " Examine yourselves, whether ye be in the faith; prove your own selves. Know ye not your own selves, how that Jesus Christ

5

is in you, except ye be reprobates?" 2 Cor. 13:5.

We know that no *man* can enter into and abide in another man, but it is not difficult for the child of God, instructed by the Spirit, to understand the possibility of the actual indwelling of Christ. He walked the paths of earth in former days, clothed in human flesh. Today, through His divine representative, the Holy Spirit, He enters into the yielded life and takes up His abode.

Indeed, the blessed Saviour even now waits outside the door, and pleads for the invitation to enter: "Behold, I stand at the door, and knock: if any man hear My voice, and open the door, I will come in to him." Rev. 3:20.

But it may not appear so clear to some how they can be "in Christ." This is a favorite expression with Paul, occurring in his epistles more than seventy times. Six of the epistles are addressed to the saints and faithful who are "in Christ."

In the first chapter of Ephesians he enumerates some of the blessings secured to those who are in Christ, declaring that "in Him" they are blessed, chosen, accepted, redeemed, heirs, united, and sealed with the Holy Spirit.

It is evident that while Christ enters into His children as a divine, living personality, He also surrounds them as a heavenly atmosphere. It is thus that He becomes a wall of separation between every true believer and the world, and He not only separates, but protects, so that no evil influence from without can harm him.

The diver puts on his specially prepared suit, and goes down into the water, an element in which he could not live. But he is surrounded with an element which is continually supplied and renewed from above, and which preserves his life.

In a similar way the child of God is born from above, and his home is there. But for the present he is in this earthly element in which he cannot live. His life therefore depends absolutely upon that which is continually supplied from above. That element is Jesus Christ.

The plant could not live out of the earth, for that is its element. The fish could not live out of water, for that is its natural element. The bird cannot live under water, for the air is its element. So the child of God who has been born from above, delivered from the power of darkness, and translated into the kingdom of His dear Son, can live in this world of sin only by abiding in that element provided from above for his existence. And this is the secret of the great deliverance from sin and the transformation of the life of a true Christian.

" The Father's presence encircled Christ, and nothing befell Him but that which Infinite Love permitted for the blessing of the world. Here was His source of comfort, and it is for us. He who is imbued with the Spirit of Christ abides in Christ. The blow that is aimed at him falls upon the Saviour, *who surrounds him with His presence.* Whatever comes to him comes from Christ. He has no need to resist evil; for Christ is his defense. Nothing can touch him except by our Lord's permission."—" *The Mount of Blessing,*" *p. 110.*

" If a piece of iron could speak, what could it say of itself? 'I am black; I am cold; I am hard.' But put it in the furnace, and what a change takes place! It has not ceased to be iron; but the blackness is gone, the coldness is gone, and the hardness is gone! It has entered into a new experience. The fire and the iron are still distinct, and yet how complete is the union! They are one. If the iron could speak, it could not glory in itself, but in the fire that makes and keeps it a bright and glowing mass.

" So must it be with the believer. Do you ask him what he is in himself? He answers, 'I am carnal, sold under sin!' For left to himself, this inevitably follows; he is brought into captivity to the law of sin which is in his members. But it is his privilege to enter into fellowship with Christ, and in Him to abide. And there *in Him* who is our life, our purity, and our power — *in Him* whose spirit can penetrate into every part of our being, the believer is no longer carnal, but spiritual; no longer overcome by sin and brought into captivity, but set free from the law of sin and death, and preserved in a condition of deliverance. This blessed experience of emancipation from sin's service and power implies a momentary and continuous act of abiding."— *Hopkins.*

There is another sense in which the expression " in Christ " is used, which is of the greatest significance to the child of God:

" Blessed be the God and Father of our Lord Jesus Christ, who hath blessed us with all spiritual blessings in heavenly things *in Christ.*" Eph. 1:3, margin. All the blessings that divine wisdom and love could provide are bestowed upon us " in Christ."

The Saviour said, " These things have I spoken unto you, that *in Me* ye might have peace." John 16:33.

The apostle Paul wrote, " Thanks be unto God, which always causeth us to triumph *in Christ.*" 2 Cor. 2:14.

John the beloved declares, " God hath given to us eternal life, and this life is *in His Son.*" 1 John 5:11.

Furthermore he says, "He that hath the Son hath life; and he that hath not the Son of God hath not life." Verse 12.

Failure to apprehend this wonderful truth means proportionate failure in the Christian experience.

In Christ is life. Possessing Christ, the believer has eternal life; but without Him there is no life. This is equally true of every other blessing of God.

Man of himself not only has no life, but he has no peace, no victory, no faith, no righteousness, nor any other attribute of God. The Father has gathered up all the blessings of infinite love, and bestowed them upon us in the precious gift of His Son. Nothing has been withheld. All is embraced and included in the one great gift.

Is it not strange that everywhere men are praying and pleading for what has already been graciously given? They pray for peace, but the Father answers, "I have already bestowed My peace upon you in Christ. Receive Him, and you have all peace." Men pray for life, and the reply is the same, "I have given you eternal life. It is in My Son. Receive Him, and you have life." Men cry to God for victory, and the answer is, "There is no victory for humanity except in the Victor."

Christ took our humanity, and won everlasting victory, not for Himself, but for men. In the same way that life and peace are gifts, so is victory a gift. " Thanks be to God, which *giveth* us the victory." 1 Cor. 15 : 57. Why do men struggle and fight to obtain what comes as a gift in Christ? They talk of victory on this point and victory on that point, when if they would only believe it, Christ is the victory on every point.

It is not some new gift from God that we need; it is a better understanding of the fact that He has already given us everything *in Christ*. It is laying hold by faith of the blessings which are already ours in Him.

" By faith you became Christ's, and by faith you are to grow up in Him,— by giving and taking. You are to *give* all,— your heart, your will, your service,— give yourself to Him to obey all His requirements; and you must *take* all,— Christ, the fulness of all blessing, to abide in your heart, to be your strength, your righteousness, your everlasting helper,— to give you power to obey."—*" Steps to Christ," p. 70.*

How many there are who have given all to God! They have made a full surrender to Him and desire only to do His will. Yet they are often filled with disappointment because of conscious lack and failure. The secret of this failure is here disclosed. They have *given* all, but they have not *taken* all.

O for faith to lay hold of this as a blessed reality!

> " Christ, the fulness of all blessing,
>   To abide in your heart,
>   To be your strength,
>   Your righteousness,
>   Your everlasting helper,
>   To give you power to obey."

The Seeker Sought

" BECAUSE I seek Thee not, O seek Thou me;
    Because my lips are dumb, O hear the cry
    I do not utter as Thou passest by,
And from my lifelong bondage set me free.

" Because content I perish far from Thee,
    O seize me, snatch me from my fate, and try
    My soul in Thy consuming fire. Draw nigh,
And let me, blinded, Thy salvation see.

" If I were pouring at Thy feet my tears,
    If I were clamoring to see Thy face,
        I should not need Thee, Lord, as now I need,
Whose dumb, dead soul knows neither hopes nor fears,
    Nor dreads the outer darkness of this place —
        Because I seek not, pray not, give Thou heed."

The Law of Growth

IT is a physical law recognized by every one that growth is produced by partaking of food. It is also understood that there is good, wholesome, nutritious food that produces a healthy growth, and there is much so-called food that is unwholesome and even injurious. Most people can easily apply the theory of this to spiritual things. The chief difficulty is that so many have acquired perverted appetites, both physical and spiritual, by indulging in the injurious food. To restore the normal appetite and feed the spiritual life so as to produce vigorous growth, is one of the most vital problems of Christian experience.

The Saviour said, " Man shall not live by bread alone, but by every word that proceedeth out of the mouth of God." Matt. 4: 4.

Of course, man can live physically by bread or material food, but there is a higher life than the mere animal. There is a spiritual realm into which a man may enter and have fellowship and communion with God. With the spiritual faculties of the soul he may feel and hear and see God, and enjoy eternal life with Him day by day. This life cannot be sustained by bread alone. It must feed upon the word of God.

In order to appreciate this, it is necessary to understand the nature of that word. It is a living word.

" God's message is full of life and power, and is keener than the sharpest two-edged sword. It pierces even to the severance of soul from spirit, and penetrates between the joints and the marrow, and it can discern the secret thoughts and purposes of the heart. And no created thing is able to escape its scrutiny." Heb. 4:12, 13 (Weymouth).

The word is living in the sense that it never dies. The words we spoke yesterday are dead and forgotten today. Most of the words of the mightiest monarchs and philosophers, poets and sages, are forgotten or known only by few. But God's word never dies and is never forgotten. It is known and loved by more people, and printed in more languages, today than ever before, though its latest page was written two thousand years ago.

It is also living in the sense that life is inherent in it and is imparted by it.

" The words that I speak unto you, they are spirit, and they are life." John 6:63.

" The life of God, which gives life to the world, is in His word."—" Gospel Workers." p. 250.

Repeatedly in the Scriptures the word is likened to a seed. When one looks at a grain of wheat, he does not see any indication of life. But if the grain is planted in the ground, soon a green leaf is seen pushing up through the soil. It has sprung up out of the life in that tiny seed. The truth concerning Jesus Christ is the seed of everlasting life. When this seed is planted in the mind and heart, it springs up and produces a new life, and this life is, like the seed, divine.

The germination and growth of this divine seed are described in the Bible, and indicate the steps by which a sinner becomes a true child of God.

The first indication of the germination of the living word, we speak of as " conviction." Paul says the word of God is " a discerner of the thoughts and intents of the heart." Heb. 4: 12.

When Peter preached the word on the day of Pentecost, the people " were pricked in their heart, and said unto Peter and to the rest of the apostles, Men and brethren, what shall we do? " Acts 2: 37.

When the prophet Jonah preached the word of God to the great heathen city of Nineveh, with all its wealth and pride and sensual idolatry, it produced conviction of sin that resulted in one of the greatest miracles of all time.

"Word came unto the king of Nineveh, and he arose from his throne, and he laid his robe from him, and covered him with sackcloth, and sat in ashes. And he caused it to be proclaimed and published through Nineveh by the decree of the king and his nobles, saying, Let neither man nor beast, herd nor flock, taste anything: let them not feed, nor drink water: but let man and beast be covered with sackcloth, and cry mightily unto God: yea, let them turn every one from his evil way, and from the violence that is in their hands." Jonah 3: 6-8.

Many times men are convicted by the word of God, but refuse to acknowledge their sins and accept repentance. But where they respond to conviction by genuine repentance and confession, the word produces in their hearts a living faith in the One who can deliver the transgressor from the guilt and power of sin.

"So then faith cometh by hearing, and hearing by the word of God." Rom. 10: 17.

Many complain of a lack of faith, and resolve to remedy the defect by spending more time in devotion or in missionary work; but the real need is more of the word of God.

"Faith that enables us to receive God's gifts is itself a gift, of which some measure is imparted to every human being. It grows as exercised in appropriating the word of God. In order to strengthen faith, we must often bring it in contact with the word."—"*Education,*" *pp. 253, 254.*

The next step in the miraculous working of the word is regeneration. "Being born again, not of corruptible seed, but of incorruptible, by the word of God, which liveth and abideth forever." 1 Peter 1:23. By the "simple act of believing God, a new life is begotten" in the heart.

A story is told of an infidel who decided to read the Bible through in order to be able to quote it more intelligently. One day he suddenly stopped reading and said, "Wife, if this book is right, we are wrong." After reading on for some time, he stopped again, saying, "Wife, if this book is right, we are lost." Still later he stopped and with deep emotion said, "Wife, if this book is right, we can be saved."

Nice story

Surely it is a wonderful word which, when applied to the vilest soul, produces conviction, faith, and regeneration.

It is this word which cleanses the heart and keeps it pure in an atmosphere charged with every form of vice and evil. "Wherewithal shall a young man cleanse his way? by taking heed thereto according to Thy word." Ps. 119:9.

When this holy word is cherished in the heart, when it is the subject of conversation and meditation, it preoccupies the ground, and leaves no room for sin. "Thy word have I hid in mine heart, that I might not sin against Thee." Ps. 119:11.

The word is also indispensable to spiritual growth. As a parting word to his dear children in the faith at Ephesus, Paul said: "And now, brethren, I commend you to God, and to the word of His grace, which is able to build you up." Acts 20:32.

How many church members there are who never grow up, but remain babes or spiritual dwarfs, simply because they do not feed upon the living word. Evidently such were the believers at Corinth:

"I, brethren, could not speak unto you as unto spiritual, but as unto carnal, even as unto babes in Christ. I have fed you with milk, and not with meat: for hitherto ye were not able to bear it, neither yet now are ye able." 1 Cor. 3:1, 2. "Every one that useth milk is unskilful in the word of righteousness: for he is a babe." Heb. 5:13.

Is it not strange that so many professed Christians neglect the diligent study of the Bible, since it is the living medium through which every essential element of the Christian life is produced? Men traverse the world, and spend time and money and life seeking what is right at hand in the Scriptures. The prophet of old said: "Thy words were found, and I did eat them; and Thy word was unto me the joy and rejoicing of mine heart." Jer. 15:16.

The joy produced by the mighty transformations of character and the precious promises for the eternal future, are not like the fleeting joys of this world. They are not affected by place or circumstances, nor by the passing of time. That joy may be found today as rich and full as by the prophet twenty-five centuries ago.

A much longer chapter than this would be needed to tell of all the miracles wrought by this living and powerful word. At least one more must be presented in this discussion.

"They that sow in tears shall reap in joy. He that goeth forth and weepeth, bearing precious seed, shall doubtless come again with rejoicing, bringing his sheaves with him." Ps. 126:5, 6.

Many seem to suppose that the power to win souls is a mysterious gift imparted only to ministers or a favored few of the elect. But the real power to save men is in the word of God. The farmer sows the seed, but he cannot make it grow and produce a harvest. The life is in the seed. So it is with the seed of everlasting life. It contains the same divine power, whether sown by the gray-haired minister, or the little child; the cultured scholar, or the humble and unlearned believer. It is only required that the sower be conscious of the sacredness of his ministry; that he love the lost enough to weep over them; and that he show by his own life that this divine, incorruptible seed produces conviction, faith, regeneration, cleansing, growth, and joy.

The Divine Surprise

THE night was long, and the shadows spread
  As far as the eye could see;
I stretched my hands to a human Christ,
  And He walked through the dark with me.

Out of the dimness at last we came,
  Our feet on the dawn-warmed sod,
And I saw by the light in His wondrous eyes,
  I walked with the Son of God.
                              — *Bertha Gerneaux Davis.*

Sanctification

WHEN a man receives Christ by faith, he is "as a child born into the kingdom of God." In the Scriptures he is spoken of as a "babe in Christ." Means have been provided by which he is to grow up unto the full stature of manhood in Christ.

This does not mean that he is growing into holiness, but rather in holiness.

"The believer does not get disentangled from the sin gradually. He breaks with it in Christ once for all; he is placed by a decisive act of the will in the sphere of perfect holiness; and it is within it that the gradual renewing of the personal life goes forward. This second gospel paradox, sanctification by faith, rests on the first, justification by faith."—"*The Way of Deliverance*," p. 10.

As we seek to appropriate day by day the blessings that are in Christ for us, there is a constant growth and expansion of the spiritual powers. The capacity to see and feel and understand the things of God is constantly increased.

As in the natural realm the first means of growth is food, so it is in the spiritual realm. "As newborn babes, desire the sincere milk of

the word, that ye may grow thereby." 1 Peter
2: 2.

Some question how it can be possible for one
to abide in Christ, permitting Christ to live in
him and control all his words and actions, and
yet make constant progress. This is easily ex-
plained. The new birth is likened to the germination of a seed that has been planted in
the soil.

" The germination of the seed represents the
beginning of spiritual life, and the development
of the plant is a beautiful figure of Christian
growth. As in nature, so in grace; there can be
no life without growth. A plant must either
grow or die. As its growth is silent and im-
perceptible, but continuous, so is the development of the Christian life. At every stage of
development our life may be perfect; yet if
God's purpose for us is fulfilled, there will be
continual advancement. Sanctification is the
work of a lifetime."—" Christ's Object Lessons,"
page 65.

This does not mean that a certain number of
years are required for sanctification. It may
be just as complete in a very short lifetime as in
a very long lifetime. It simply means that there
is to be no cessation of growth — no stagnation,
but continuous life and vigor in the Christian
experience.

"Let a living faith run like threads of gold through the performance of even the smallest duties. Then all the daily work will promote Christian growth. There will be a continual looking unto Jesus. Love for Him will give vital force to everything that is undertaken. Thus through the right use of our talents, we may link ourselves by a golden chain to the higher world. This is true sanctification; for sanctification consists in the cheerful performance of daily duties in perfect obedience to the will of God."— *Id., p. 360.*

Some confusion may be avoided by noting the various aspects of sanctification presented in the Scriptures.

"Such were some of you: but ye are washed, but ye are sanctified, but ye are justified in the name of the Lord Jesus, and by the Spirit of our God." 1 Cor. 6:11.

Sanctification is often spoken of as if it meant cleansing, but here the meaning is made very clear. Sanctification as here used means set apart or dedicated unto God. Cleansing is separation *from sin,* but sanctification is separation *unto God.* It is in this sense that the Saviour used the word regarding Himself: "For their sakes I sanctify Myself, that they also might be sanctified through the truth." John 17:19.

Here sanctification is an act, but in other places in the Scriptures it is represented as a process.

"The very God of peace sanctify you wholly; and I pray God your whole spirit and soul and body be preserved blameless unto the coming of our Lord Jesus Christ." 1 Thess. 5:23.

"Sanctification is the work, not of a day, or of a year, but of a lifetime. The struggle for conquest over self, for holiness and heaven, is a lifelong struggle. Without continual effort and constant activity, there can be no advancement in the divine life, no attainment of the victor's crown."—"Testimonies," Vol. VIII, pp. 312, 313.

In these statements sanctification is represented first as an act and then as a process. But there is still another aspect of the subject which makes it complete by presenting sanctification as a person. "Of Him are ye in Christ Jesus, who of God is made unto us wisdom, and righteousness, and sanctification, and redemption." 1 Cor. 1:30.

It is only as we view sanctification under these three aspects that it becomes a harmonious whole. Having renounced all connection with sin and self, and yielded our lives in solemn dedication to be possessed by the Lord Jesus Christ, to be lived wholly unto God, we experience sanctification as an *act*.

In the continual turning of our back upon our own works and looking to the indwelling Christ to live His own life, both willing and doing His own pleasure in us, we experience the *process* of sanctification.

Recognizing that there is no good thing in ourselves, and so losing our lives and appropriating Christ that we can truly say with Paul, " It is no longer I that live, but Christ that liveth in me," we have sanctification as a *person*.

When a little child fully surrenders to Jesus, it does not make the child appear like a mature man, but like a Christlike child. Later he may be a Christlike youth, and finally a Christlike man. So when one is born as a little child into the kingdom of God, there will be the revelation of Christ in childlike perfection, day by day growing and developing in all the Christian graces to full maturity in Christ.

I KNOW

I KNOW not where God's lilies fair unfold
   Their pure white petals in eternal light;
I know not where the daisy's heart of gold
   Ne'er feels the chilling dews of autumn's night.

I know not where the sunlit mountains rise
   In their calm beauty, till they almost seem
To melt into the blue of summer skies,
   And crown the brightness of the peaceful dream.

I know not where life's river sweeps along
   That " maketh glad the city of our God,"
Or where the " many voices " sing the song
   Along the ways that angels oft have trod.

But somewhere in the starry realms of space
   Is heaven, with its holy age of rest;
I only know that I shall see His face;
   And this, of all my joy, will be the best.

                           — Mrs. M. A. Holt.

Sent from God

" There was a man sent from God, whose name was John." " He was a burning and a shining light." John 1 : 6; 5 : 35.

" Then went out to him Jerusalem, and all Judea, and all the region round about Jordan, and were baptized of him in Jordan, confessing their sins." Matt. 3 : 5, 6.

Here is an example of a marvelously successful ministry, the secret of which may easily be overlooked.

This great harvest of souls did not come as a result of high attainments in worldly scholarship. Nor did it come as the culmination of many long years of an increasingly successful ministry.

A man was *sent from God.* He was a burning and a shining light. Thousands flocked to him and were converted.

We have an equally striking testimony concerning Christ, and also concerning ourselves.

" Jesus saith unto them, My meat is to do the will of *Him that sent Me,* and to finish His work." John 4 : 34.

The consciousness of the fact that He was *sent from God* seemed never absent from His mind, and is expressed about thirty-five times in thirteen chapters of the book of John. Let us study a few of these statements:

" I seek not Mine own will, but the will of the Father which hath sent Me." John 5: 30.

" My doctrine is not Mine, but His that sent Me." John 7: 16.

" I know Him: for I am from Him; and He hath sent Me." John 7: 29.

" Yet a little while am I with you, and then I go unto Him that sent Me." John 7: 33.

" I am not alone, but I and the Father that sent Me." John 8: 16.

" He that sent Me is true; and I speak to the world those things which I have heard of Him." John 8: 26.

" I proceeded forth and came from God; neither came I of Myself, but He sent Me." John 8: 42.

" I must work the works of Him that sent Me, while it is day." John 9: 4.

" He that seeth Me seeth Him that sent Me." John 12: 45.

" I have not spoken of Myself; but the Father which sent Me, He gave Me a commandment, what I should say, and what I should speak." John 12: 49.

There was not the slightest uncertainty in the mind of Christ on these two points: He was sent from God, and He had a definite work to do for God.

Obviously, this should be the ruling motive in the lives of all Christ's disciples. A mere kindly disposition toward the unfortunate, or sympathy for those in need, or a conviction that one ought to help the lost, is inadequate. Since the word of God is positive and explicit and personal, there must be a divine certainty on the part of the one called.

When praying to our Father, the Saviour said, "As Thou hast *sent Me into the world, even so have I also sent them into the world.*" John 17:18.

Later, in speaking directly to His disciples, He said, "As My Father hath sent Me, even so send I you." John 20:21.

Christ was certain that He was sent of God into the world for a definite work. We have equal grounds for certainty that we are sent of Christ into the world for a definite work. How frequently and in how many ways has the Lord emphasized this truth!

"Not more surely is the place prepared for us in the heavenly mansions than is the special place designated on earth where we are to work for God."—"*Christ's Object Lessons,*" *p. 327.*

Closely allied to the question of Christ's being sent from God into the world, was the question

6

of His relation to this world as the messenger of God.

"Then said Jesus again unto them, I go My way, and ye shall seek Me, and shall die in your sins: whither I go, ye cannot come. Then said the Jews, Will He kill Himself? because He saith, Whither I go, ye cannot come. And He said unto them, *Ye are from beneath; I am from above: ye are of this world; I am not of this world.* I said therefore unto you, that ye shall die in your sins." John 8: 21-24.

How striking and significant are those words! You are of this world; I am not of this world. You are from beneath; I am from above.

Again in His prayer to the Father the Saviour, in the most definite and personal way, includes His disciples with Himself: "They are not of the world, even as I am not of the world." John 17: 16.

And in directly addressing them, He said: "If ye were of the world, the world would love his own: but because *ye are not of the world,* but I have chosen you out of the world, therefore the world hateth you." John 15: 19.

With a little thought one can see plainly why the conviction that He is not of this world belongs with the conviction that He is sent of God. One who is "of this world" cannot help the world. It is because He is "from above" that

He has power to rescue those " from beneath."
A man rows out to sea in a lifeboat to rescue
some shipwrecked mariners. If the men struggling in the water could rescue themselves, he
would have no mission there. What folly, then,
for him to cast himself into the sea! His power
to save lies in the fact that he is not in the water
with them, but in the lifeboat.

Our power as Christ's disciples to save men
in the world lies in the fact that we are from
above, and not of this world. What folly, then,
for a professed disciple to attempt work for
God while compromising with the world! Many
seem to think that the more closely they can af-
filiate with the world while still professing to be
Christians, the better they can win men; but
the very opposite is true, as the Saviour Himself
taught.

Christ seemed never to be unconscious of these
two vital facts, and often declared them publicly: " I do not belong here. I am from above.
My only reason for being here is that I am sent
from God to save men. When that work is done,
I shall return to Him." How profoundly such
a conviction would affect the lives and ministry
of all Christ's disciples!

Imagine a representative of the Red Cross
on a mission of mercy to a country ravaged by
war, pestilence, starvation, and death. He is

supplied with abundant means to treat the sick, and to clothe and feed the perishing. But he feels that he can accomplish more for the people by becoming as much like them as possible. He neglects the care of his health, and goes half clothed and half fed, ragged and unclean. How he would dishonor the glorious country and principles he is supposed to represent! Instead of saving people, many would be lost because of his misguided course, who might have been saved if he had rightly fulfilled his mission.

Christ's disciples are to be a peculiar people; in this world, but not of the world. They are to be citizens and representatives of the heavenly world and dispensers of heavenly treasure. John was only a man, but he was "sent from God." That gave him the assurance of God's presence and power. It made him invincible. It brought the multitudes to him. It clothed him with power to present truth that convicted and converted sinners.

It is a great thing to be sent from God, and to know it. And it is a great thing to abandon oneself utterly to God's mission.

Every true disciple should be able to answer these questions at any time with deep conviction and divine certainty: Why are you here? Because Christ sent me. What are you doing? I am doing the will of Him that sent me. What are you teaching by word and life? I am teaching only what He has taught me and given me to teach.

Many seem to overlook the fact that the very foundation of service is believing on Jesus. Service is deeper and broader than mere human activity.

"Then said they unto Him, What shall we do, that we might work the works of God? Jesus answered and said unto them, This is the work of God, that ye believe on Him whom He hath sent." John 6: 28, 29.

The highest service John could render to God was to believe on Jesus — believe that he himself was sent from God as the forerunner of Christ.

If we know by experience the joy and satisfaction of acceptance in the Beloved, how can we do any less?

My Prayer

O THAT my eyes might closèd be
To what becomes me not to see;
That deafness might possess my ear
To what concerns me not to hear;
That truth my tongue might always tie
From ever speaking foolishly;
That no vain thought might ever rest
Or be conceived within my breast;
Wash, Lord, and purify my heart,
And make me clean in every part;
And when 'tis clean, Lord, keep it so,
For that is more than I can do.

— *Thomas Ellwood.*

THOUGH He is so bright and we are so dim,
We are made in His image to witness Him.

— *Robert Browning.*

THOU hast but this, to set thy feet where Mine
Make prints, step after step, a track for thine.

— *Margaret Sangster.*

Winning Souls

WE have constantly to remind ourselves that the religion of Christ is utterly unselfish. I am not to think that Jesus died for me that I might have peace and happiness here and heaven hereafter; but He saves me that I may share with Him in the work of saving other sinners.

The call of God to soul-winning work is specific and personal. He says to all His disciples, "Follow Me, and I will make you fishers of men." Matt. 4:19.

"The relations between God and each soul are as distinct and full as though there were not another soul upon the earth to share His watchcare, not another soul for whom He gave His beloved Son."—"Steps to Christ," p. 100.

Let us keep this intensely personal relationship in mind while we notice some of the Saviour's teaching.

"A certain man had two sons; and he came to the first, and said, Son, go work today in my vineyard. He answered and said, I will not: but afterward he repented, and went. And he came to the second, and said likewise. And he answered and said, I go, sir: and went not.

127

Whether of them twain did the will of his father?" Matt. 21: 28-31.

Evidently these two sons represent two classes which include all who profess to be children of God. We need to be very clear about the four points involved in the command, and the fact that not to obey *all four* is not to obey at all.

GO — WORK — TODAY — IN MY VINEYARD

Another parable makes plain the definite work required of each disciple:

"A certain man made a great supper, and bade many: and sent his servant at suppertime to say to them that were bidden, Come; for all things are now ready." Luke 14: 16, 17.

With this parable the Lord unfolded His plan for saving the lost. The great invitation is to be given to every " nation, kindred, tongue, and people," and the Lord sends " His servant " to carry the good news. The servant gave the message, but those invited, " with one consent began to make excuse."

Then the master said to his servant, " Go out quickly into the streets and lanes of the city, and bring in hither the poor, and the maimed, and the halt, and the blind." And the servant said, " Lord, it is done as thou hast commanded."

Happy indeed is that servant who can say this to the heavenly Master with confidence.

WINNING SOULS 129

And the lord said unto the servant, " Go out into the highways and hedges, and compel them to come in, that my house may be filled." The servant is not only commissioned to extend the invitation, but has authority from on high to compel them to come. Men can compel with the force of physical might, but the only compelling power in the moral universe is the power of love. The servant of God must needs learn as did the great apostle Paul, that " love never fails." 1 Cor. 13 : 8 (Weymouth).

Again, the Saviour said, " Ye have not chosen Me, but I have chosen you, and ordained you, that ye should go and bring forth fruit, and that your fruit should remain." John 15 : 16.

Since these scriptures teach so clearly that " every true disciple is born into the kingdom of God as a missionary," is it not strange that so few professed disciples are real soul-winners?

The Lord not only calls every believer to this work, but He places upon each a definite responsibility for the lost.

" When I say unto the wicked, O wicked man, thou shalt surely die; if thou dost not speak to warn the wicked from his way, that wicked man shall die in his iniquity; *but his blood will I require at thine hand.*" Eze. 33 : 8.

" The Saviour's commission to the disciples included all the believers. It includes all believers in Christ to the end of time. . . . Whatever one's calling in life, his first interest should be to win souls for Christ."—" *The Desire of Ages*," *page 822.*

It is not even possible to occupy a neutral position, professing to be Christians, yet not actually and actively seeking to save souls; for Christ declared, "He that is not with Me is against Me; and he that gathereth not with Me scattereth abroad." Matt. 12:30.

There may be those who will say, "I cannot work successfully for people when I have no burden for them, but have a great aversion for that kind of work."

This is true, but it is also true that one cannot be saved and remain indifferent to the unsaved. If one has no concern for the lost, it is quite conclusive evidence that he himself has only an empty profession. When Christ calls one to be His disciple, He makes that one a fisher of men. He not only places upon him the responsibility of winning souls, but gives him a burden for the unsaved.

"I say the truth in Christ, I lie not, my conscience also bearing me witness in the Holy Ghost, that I have great heaviness and continual sorrow in my heart. For I could wish that myself were accursed from Christ for my brethren, my kinsmen according to the flesh." Rom. 9:1-3.

Recognizing as from God the call, the responsibility, and the burden, every true disciple is eager to learn the best and most effective means and methods of soul-winning service.

First, it is well to remember that the most successful worker must ever be progressing in skill and efficiency. The young graduate from a medical college may have all the theory, but it is the experience which counts. At the end of each year he should know better how to diagnose and treat all manner of diseases. So it is with the physician of the soul.

Many are perplexed about how to start in this work, regarding it as something mysterious and difficult. If they will but study the methods of Christ, they will find it simple and easy. In His dealing with the Samaritan woman, He shows how a request for a drink may introduce a conversation that ends in the salvation of a soul.

And the amazing thing is, that a poor half-heathen woman, notorious for her impure life, could be the instrument the very same day of bringing to Jesus many of the people who knew all about her life. How can any one today excuse himself from personal work for souls on the ground that he himself is not good enough or has not been a Christian long enough? The Scripture gives instance after instance of converts who went out and won others to Christ on the very day they found Him for themselves.

There are three facts the personal worker must on no account lose sight of:

1. His own life must be right.
2. He must know and use the Scriptures.
3. He must pray.

It is not logical to suppose that one who is cherishing any known sin in his own life would be used of God to win souls. It is true that men who were harboring secret sin have preached the word and souls have been saved, but they were saved in spite of the preacher, and no credit will be given to him. After all, the greatest appeal a man can make is the appeal of his own life — the evidence of a divine power working in his life and delivering him from sin.

Then one must know the truth and constantly use the sword of the Spirit, which is the word of God. It is a safe rule to avoid argument, and to rely more upon the power of the word than human logic or reasoning. Many a man has found Christ because the worker refused to argue with him.

Finally, the believer who attempts personal work without much prayer will be certain to fail. He must prevail with God first in order to prevail with men. But glorious miracles await those who will meet the conditions, claim the promise, and persevere in prayer.

" This is the confidence that we have in Him, that, if we ask anything according to His will, He heareth us: and if we know that He hear us, whatsoever we ask, we know that we have the petitions that we desired of Him. If any man see his brother sin a sin which is not unto death, he shall ask, and he shall give him life for them that sin not unto death." 1 John 5 : 14-16.

I remember a woman whose daughter ran away from her home and family and plunged into the depths of sin. She was stricken with a terrible disease, and brought home to her mother to die. Her soul seemed filled with bitterness toward God and man, and every appeal to confess her sins brought only scorn and cursing. The mother's distress was great, but she staked everything on the above promise, and day and night she cried to God. The girl's sufferings were indescribable, and the end seemed near. One day the mother knelt by the bedside, and clasping her daughter in her arms, she wrestled with God with a mighty faith, like Jacob of old. And the demon was dethroned. The girl sent for her husband and children, confessed to them and to God with deepest contrition of heart, and died. How many more souls we might win to Christ if we would only really pray!

The Privilege and Necessity of Prayer

Do you pray? This may be an unusual question, but it is certainly a very vital one. The necessity for prayer is taken for granted, yet if the truth were known, it would be surprising to find how many of those whose names are on the church book do not pray.

I asked a young friend who has been all her life among Christian people, " Do you pray? "

She answered, " No."

" Have you never said any prayer at all? "

" Yes, I suppose I have prayed four or five times in the last ten years."

How strange that intelligent beings should be born in a Christian land where from childhood they hear of God, live a lifetime, and die without talking to their Creator! He gives them life, health, food, clothing, and friends. They breathe His air, enjoy His sunshine and rain, birds and flowers, sea and land. They see and experience a thousand evidences of His power and countless tokens of His love, yet they do not talk with Him. They do not thank Him for His unfailing kindness, nor seek Him for His help.

But the question in which we are particularly interested is: Do *you* pray?

Prayer is absolutely essential to spiritual life. One might be saved, and not read the Bible. He might be blind, or unable to read. One might be saved without going to church. He might be where there was no church, or an invalid who could not attend public service. But if he is saved, he must pray. Prayer is the cry of the soul to God. Even the thief suffering and dying on the cross prayed, and his prayer was answered. In the statement of the conditions on which God promises to save men, prayer comes first: " Seek ye the Lord while He may be found, call ye upon Him while He is near." Isa. 55: 6.

Do you neglect anything on which all your *earthly* prosperity depends, as lightly as you do prayer? In these days most people are convinced of the importance of education, and great effort and sacrifice are made to secure it. Are you seeking to develop a broad, well-disciplined, noble mind? If so, you cannot afford to neglect prayer.

Do you have friends and acquaintances whom you love, and over whom you desire to exert an influence for good? You cannot do this without prayer.

Have you some talent, some natural gift, which places you in a position of strong leadership?

Prayer will determine largely whether this will prove a blessing or a curse.

Have you means at your command for which you are responsible and the expenditure of which requires wisdom and judgment? How can you meet these responsibilities without disastrous mistakes, unless you pray? You know that the judgments of God are in the land, and thinking men and women believe that great and solemn events are just before us. In view of these things, do you pray?

I do not ask whether you *say* your prayers. I do not ask if occasionally you make a formal call upon God, nor if you respond when asked to open a public service with prayer. I do not ask if you cry to God when some great crisis overtakes you, and you stand in the presence of disaster or death. I ask, Do you pray? Do you converse with God as friend with friend? Do you look up into His face, and whisper words which you want no human ear to hear, and which He alone can understand? Do you linger in sweet communion with Him, like a lover at the gate, reluctant to say farewell, and cherishing as unspeakably precious every moment alone with Him? Would you rather miss food or work or study or friends or rest than the quiet hour with Him? Do you hurry away from human society when your duties are done, that you may enjoy the sweet companionship, the comfort, the counsel, the reproof, the love of your Saviour? Do you pray?

Why should we pray? Our first answer to this question may well be, "Because there is a God." Man is by nature a worshiping being. He will worship, and both the Scriptures and human experience show that he becomes like what he worships.

Among the elements which constitute real prayer to God are worship, praise, confession, petition, and intercession. It requires no argument to show that it is reasonable and for their own best interest for men to worship God. The worship of the Creator produces a noble and beautiful character in contrast to degradation, ignorance, superstition, and sensuality, which result from the worship of anything but the true God.

One of the fundamental elements of a beautiful character is gratitude. One is considered rude and selfish who does not express or manifest gratitude for the little common courtesies of life. Yet we all revel in the pure air, sunshine, rain, birds, flowers, fruits, and a thousand beauties of nature and joys of life, for which we expend no effort or care, but which come as loving gifts from God. He also provides the necessities — food, clothing, health, home, friends, protection; and beyond the material numberless blessings, He gives peace, rest, and happiness to those who fear Him. Who can help but sing His praise, and express continual gratitude and thanks to Him? This is why we pray.

We are in a world where sin has entered as an intruder. We have all suffered inexpressibly, but God has suffered most of all. Sin is rebellion in His home, and results in destruction to some of His children. Infinite love constrained Him to give His Son as a substitute to suffer the penalty of sin for every sinner. Having paid the penalty, He offers eternal life to each one who will meet the conditions.

One condition is that man fully and freely acknowledge his guilt, and make confession of his sins. This is why we pray, confessing our iniquities and transgressions to the One who alone can and will cleanse us from sin.

Sin robs us of all spiritual blessings, and oppresses us in numberless ways, materially as well as spiritually. God has infinite resources to supply our every need, and He has chosen to establish a very intimate relationship between Himself and His children, by supplying their needs in response to their petitions. " All things, whatsoever ye shall ask in prayer, believing, ye shall receive." Matt. 21: 22. So we pray because we are conscious of need. One who never really prays is saying by his course, " I do not need God. I can get along without Him. The things I desire most I can obtain without His help."

The story is told of a little girl whose way led through a dark wood. On entering it she prayed for the Lord to keep her from harm, and on reaching the other side she said, " Thank you, Lord; now I can go the rest of the way alone." The story is probably not true, for a little child who trusted God enough to call upon Him for help, would want Him to go all the way. But does not the story illustrate the attitude of many? Could we not all truly say, " When I become careless or negligent about prayer, I soon find I am drifting; my experience is most satisfactory when I pray most earnestly and often "?

God says, " Call upon Me in the day of trouble: I will deliver thee, and thou shalt glorify Me." Ps. 50 : 15. Do you ever have any trouble? Then that is one reason why you should pray.

Again He says : " Is any sick among you ? let him call for the elders of the church ; and let them pray over him, anointing him with oil in the name of the Lord : and the prayer of faith shall save the sick." James 5 : 14, 15. It is a great mistake to let physicians and nurses, treatments and sanitariums, rob us of our sense of the need of God and of prayer for the sick. God has given us means to aid nature in the restoration of the sick, but they were never intended to come between us and our Healer. So if we are ever sick, or have friends who are sick, it is another reason why we should pray.

God has made us His ambassadors to our fellow men. As such we urge His claims upon them, and then as Christ's own representatives we plead the cases of these men at the throne of grace, and urge the merits of our Master in their behalf. There is surely no greater privilege or joy than that of intercession for those who are dear to us, but who are unsaved. It is our solemn duty to represent those who are bound to us by the ties of affection or influence before the heavenly mercy-seat. And in God's great plan He has promised to do for them what He could not do if we did not pray.

So we might go over an almost endless list of reasons for prayer. Paul thus embraces them all: "In everything by prayer and supplication with thanksgiving let your requests be made known unto God. And the peace of God, which passeth all understanding, shall keep your hearts and minds through Christ Jesus." Phil. 4: 6, 7.

When, Where, and How to Pray

At one time Paul pointed out two fundamental human weaknesses, one characteristic of women and one of men. The former are warned against the adornment of the external and physical, in contrast to the inner, spiritual being. The latter he exhorts to " pray everywhere, lifting up holy hands, without wrath and doubting." 1 Tim. 2 : 8.

It is inherent in the nature of man to trust himself; and to trust self is to doubt God. The more abundant a man's supply of health, education, wealth, or talent, the greater his temptation to trust in his own endowments or possessions, and close his eyes to his need of God.

No man can truly pray who is self-sufficient, for real prayer springs from the consciousness of the soul that it is weak, inadequate, and incomplete, apart from God. God has all that man needs, and longs to supply his needs. But He can do this only on condition that man will be His friend and not His enemy. The basis of prayer, therefore, is friendship between God and man, springing from God's love to man and man's consciousness of his utter need of God, and his willingness to yield and obey God.

In view of these facts, when should a man pray? Christ taught that men should "pray always." Some men have noticed this teaching, and it is interesting to observe the result.

Daniel was a great statesman, a prime minister, standing next to the ruler of an empire embracing the known world. He started as a humble student, chosen from a group of war captives brought from a far country. Only a few years elapsed until he was second in authority over the whole empire. "Praying always," was one of the unalterable principles of his life. The prospect of loss of friends, of position, or of life itself, never caused him to waver a moment. This fellowship with God in constant prayer imparted to him such wisdom and ability and unerring judgment, that keen, unscrupulous, intriguing political enemies could find no fault with his life nor with his administration of vast responsibilities. His was a model life for every humble captive as well as for every great statesman.

Moses was another leader who figures as a giant character in the history of the world. Notice some illustrations of *when* he prayed:

When only three days' journey from Sinai, the people complained, and God sent a plague among them, so that they died. Moses prayed, and the fire was quenched. Miriam and Aaron criticized Moses, especially over domestic matters, as they did not like his wife, and they were also envious of his position. Under these circumstances Moses prayed, and his sister, who had been stricken with leprosy as a judgment for her presumption, was healed.

When the twelve spies returned from Canaan with their discouraging report, the people wept and complained; but Moses prayed. The disaffection and murmuring grew worse, and God threatened to disinherit and destroy Israel; but Moses prayed the more earnestly, and his prayers prevailed.

Then there arose a rebellion of two hundred and fifty princes, " famous in the congregation, men of renown." They determined to depose Moses as leader. Moses immediately resorted to prayer. God visited His judgments upon the leaders of the rebellion, and they were all destroyed.

The next day the whole nation rose up against Moses, saying, " Ye have killed the people of the Lord." Num. 16: 41. Again God punished the people, and again they were spared in answer to Moses' prayers. His whole life is a record of masterful leadership and noble, successful service, because he prayed always. Only three times in his career is it recorded that he acted without prayer, and each time he made a grievous mistake.

Surely one who is lacking in almost every Christian grace may well pray; but these illustrations serve to show that even one who has intellect, opportunity, power, genius, may make the most of these gifts only by being always instant in prayer.

The Bible commends public prayer in the house of God, family prayer, the united petitions of two of Christ's disciples, but above all, the unceasing prayer of the individual.

Prayer is not something to turn to only in case of danger, emergency, or crisis; it is the means of constant communication between a loving and mighty God and His needy and responsive children. Prayer is the secret door to that channel through which petitions ascend to God and help and blessing descend to men. At God's end the channel is always open. How much of the time do you keep it open at this end? When do you pray?

"I will therefore that men pray *everywhere*." 1 Tim. 2: 8.

Some people never think of praying except at the bedside, when retiring for the night. Others pray only at family worship, and still others confine their praying to the church.

I was riding along the road with a stalwart young farmer in the West. He spoke feelingly of his father, who had recently died. Pointing to the right, he said, " Do you see that field? Many a time while hoeing corn in that field with my father, he would say, ' John, let's kneel down here and pray.' And over on this side I can remember again and again, when hauling hay, he would say, ' John, I want you to be a good Christian boy and work for God. Kneel down with me while I ask the Lord to bless and keep you ! "

Tears were coursing down his cheeks as he continued, " My father was the most godly, consistent Christian I ever knew. He was always praying out in the field, in the barn, in the house, and wherever he went."

The Scripture says, " I will therefore that men pray everywhere." Is not our conception of God and our relation to Him indicated by *where* we pray? If a person is conscious of God only when he is going to bed, how much genuine religion has he? But if a person is conscious of God as his Father, his Saviour, his personal Friend, wherever he goes, then he will pray accordingly.

A person may say a prayer once a day at his bedside, and that prayer be a meaningless form. But one can hardly conceive of a person's praying *everywhere* unless the presence of God is to him a vital reality.

Hardly a day passes that does not record some great catastrophe in which human lives are lost. In the face of some awful peril, almost all intelligent people cry to God. It may be audibly or inaudibly, but there is an instinctive appeal to the only One who has omnipotent power to save.

But how different must be the cry of one whose previous prayer has been mere form, from that of one who has known and communed with God everywhere. It is like a blind man groping in the dark for something of which he is not certain.

In the Scripture we have an interesting picture of men of God praying " everywhere." Isaac prayed in the field. Elijah prayed on the top of Mt. Carmel. Elisha prayed in the chamber alone with the dead child. David prayed in his bed at night. Jonah prayed from the bowels of the great fish. Daniel prayed alone in his room. Jesus withdrew into a solitary place, and prayed; He prayed in Gethsemane, and on the cross. The disciples prayed in the upper room until Pentecost came. Peter prayed on the housetop and in the chamber of death. Paul prayed in the Philippian jail at midnight. He kneeled down with the brethren at Miletus on the seashore, and prayed. He prayed in the temple, on the sea, and in his Roman prison.

How many places on this sin-cursed and blood-stained earth have been consecrated by the prayers of saints and martyrs,— the catacombs of Rome; the rocky peaks and caves and mountain fastnesses of the Alps; the rack and the dungeon and the blazing pile; the dark jungles in the heart of Africa, where Livingstone died on his knees; the mysterious fastnesses of Madagascar and the dark habitations of cruelty and cannibalism in the islands of the sea,— all these have witnessed the prayers of heroic men and women who prayed *everywhere* to a God who is *everywhere,* and whose ear is open and His mighty hand ready to respond to the cry of sorrow and distress and need.

Though the call of the Master take us to the ends of the earth, or no farther than the circle of our own home, let us learn the precious lesson of praying everywhere.

How do you pray? How little do we discriminate between saying our prayers and really praying! How often do we say our prayers, and in ten minutes do not even remember what we said!

Is it any wonder that when a crisis or a calamity comes, and we really want help from God, we pray, and then cry in distress, " My prayers are in vain! They do not go higher than my head! God does not hear nor answer me"?

Here is a prayer by a devout servant of God that we may well analyze and endeavor to make the spirit of our hearts:

"Lord, take my heart; for I cannot give it. It is Thy property. Keep it pure, for I cannot keep it for Thee. Save me in spite of myself, my weak, unchristlike self. Mold me, fashion me, raise me into a pure and holy atmosphere, where the rich current of Thy love can flow through my soul."—"*Christ's Object Lessons,*" *p. 159.*

Reader, if you are alone, will you not get down on your knees now and begin: "Lord, take my heart; for I cannot give it"? Repeat it till the solemn truth of what you are saying is borne into your soul by the Holy Spirit. Many a time you have said, "Lord, I give you my heart," and yet you have gone on cherishing selfishness and pride in that heart which you never really gave to Him. No, my friend, your faculties are too benumbed and intoxicated by sin, your eyes are too blind, your will too weak, to really give your heart to God. Oh, implore Him now to take what you are too sinful and helpless to give. Tell Him it is your choice.

"It is Thy property." It is His because you are His; because He has given you existence, and has redeemed you from death by the sacrifice of His own life. It is dishonest, it is a crime against God and your own soul, not to let Him have that which rightfully belongs to Him, and which He values more than His life.

" Keep it pure, for I cannot keep it for Thee." Are you not convinced that you cannot keep it after your long record of desperate and heart-breaking but utterly futile efforts? Do you not know from sad experience that your heart is " deceitful above all things, and desperately wicked "?

And would you know the unutterable peace and rest of a heart kept as pure and holy as the mighty Keeper who dwells within it? Then do not try longer to keep it for Him; let Him keep it for Himself.

" Save me in spite of myself, my weak, un-christlike self." I struggle, I resolve, I determine, but " I am carnal, sold under sin." " To will is present with me; but how to perform that which is good I find not." So, Lord, I find that I am the greatest obstacle. " Save me in spite of myself — this weak, unchristlike self."

Pray on, friend, the way is growing brighter. " Mold me, fashion me, raise me into a pure and holy atmosphere, where the rich current of Thy love can flow through my soul." Is not this where your life has failed to stand the test? It

did not bear the stamp of the divine workman-
ship. *It lacked prayer.*

" By beholding we become changed." Now,
as you pray, the work is going on. As you cry
to Him, He stands by your side. He is looking
down upon your bowed head and tear-stained
face. He is raising you up into that pure and
holy atmosphere. Just be yielding. Keep the
door open wide. Let the rich current of His
love flow through your soul.

Oh, how sweet it is really to kneel at the feet
of Jesus and pray !

ONE small life in God's great plan,
   How futile it seems as the apes roll,
Do what it may, or strive how it can,
   To alter the sweep of the infinite whole!
A single stitch in an endless web,
A drop in the ocean's flow and ebb;
But the pattern is rent where the stitch is lost,
Or marred where the tangled threads have crossed;
And each life that fails of the true intent
Mars the perfect plan that its Master meant.
           — *Susan Coolidge.*

Abiding in Christ

WE can think of no more appropriate word to conclude our study of the victorious life than that of the Master Himself,

"Abide *in Me,* and I *in you.*"

The gracious promises of pardon and victory are all conditional on being *in Christ.* Our very life depends on our entering into this relationship with the living and life-giving One.

"If any man be *in Christ,* he is a new creature; old things are passed away; behold, all things are become new." 2 Cor. 5:17. One who has this experience, the Saviour says, "hath everlasting life, and shall not come into condemnation; but is passed from death unto life." John 5:24. This corresponds also to the words of Paul, "As *in Adam* all die, even so *in Christ* shall all be made alive." 1 Cor. 15:22. Life comes to us as a result of entering into Christ, and this life is His own pure and victorious life.

On the other hand, the Saviour said emphatically, "If a man abide not *in Me,* he is cast forth as a branch, and is withered; and men gather them, and cast them into the fire, and they are burned." 1 Cor. 15:6. These words imply that a man might accept Christ as his Saviour, and be *in Him,* but not abide or continue in Him, and so be cast away and lost. This is also stated in the second verse: " Every branch *in Me* that beareth not fruit He taketh away."

This experience of being *in Christ* is not one which we can gain by any effort of our own, but it is the work of our heavenly Father in response to our obedience and faith. " He which stablisheth us with you *in Christ,* and hath anointed us, is God." 2 Cor. 1:21. This very anointing of God teaches us the way, and enables us, day by day and hour by hour, to abide in Christ. " The anointing which ye have received of Him abideth in you, and ye need not that any man teach you: but as the same anointing teacheth you of all things, and is truth, and is no lie, and even as it hath taught you, ye shall *abide in Him.*" 1 John 2:27.

This wonderful experience is beautifully and forcefully expressed by Dr. A. B. Simpson when he sings, " I have learned the wondrous secret of abiding in the Lord."

> " I am crucified with Jesus,
>   And He lives and dwells in me;
> I have ceased from all my struggling,
>   'Tis no longer I, but He;
> All my will is yielded to Him,
>   And His Spirit reigns within,
> And His precious blood each moment,
>   Keeps me cleansed and free from sin.

" All my cares I cast upon Him,
    And he bears them all away;
All my fears and griefs I tell Him,
    All my needs from day to day.
All my strength I draw from Jesus,
    By His breath I live and move;
E'en His very mind He gives me,
    And His faith, and life, and love.

" For my words I take His wisdom,
    For my works His Spirit's power,
For my ways His gracious presence
    Guards and guides me ev'ry hour.
Of my heart He is the portion,
    Of my joy the ceaseless spring;
Saviour, sanctifier, keeper,
    Glorious Lord and coming King."

The result of abiding in Christ cannot be over-estimated, for this is the secret of all success in His service. So the beloved disciple writes, " He that saith he *abideth in Him* ought himself also so to walk, even as He walked." 1 John 2: 6.

What a denial of Christ it is for one professing to be His disciple to go about doing his own pleasure and following his own ways! God sent His Son into the world to save sinners. He makes the most positive claim that Jesus saves His people from their sins. How wicked and unfair it is to profess before the world to be His child, and then make " Him a liar " by living in known and habitual sin!

"Ye know that He was manifested to take away our sins; and in Him is no sin. Whosoever *abideth in Him* sinneth not." 1 John 3 : 6. We have no power to keep ourselves from sinning; but in Him is no sin, and abiding in Him, we are kept.

There are four great incentives to the believer to seek this experience of abiding in Christ:

1. " Whosoever abideth in Him sinneth not." 1 John 3 : 6.

2. " He that abideth in Me, and I in him, the same bringeth forth much fruit." John 15 : 5.

3. " If ye abide in Me, and My words abide in you, ye shall ask what ye will, and it shall be done unto you." John 15 : 7.

4. " And now, little children, abide in Him; that, when He shall appear, we may have confidence, and not be ashamed before Him at His coming." 1 John 2 : 28.

In this abiding experience lies our daily victory over sin, our ability to bring forth to His glory, our unlimited success in prayer, and our assurance of being ready to meet our King when He returns in His glory.

Let us be sure that we understand clearly how this abiding experience is secured and maintained. Many have striven earnestly to obtain it, but without success, for we have already read that it is the work of God. We must cease

striving to abide, and believe that God has " stab-
lished " us " in Christ," and will, with our consent and co-operation, maintain the relationship.
This co-operation means the exercise of faith.
" Do you ask, ' How am I to abide in Christ? '
In the same way as you received Him at first.
. . . You gave yourself to God, to be His wholly,
to serve and obey Him, and you took Christ as
your Saviour. You could not yourself atone
for your sins or change your heart; but having
given yourself to God, you believed that He for
Christ's sake did all this for you. By *faith* you
became Christ's, and by faith you are to grow up
in Him — by giving and taking. You are to
give all,— your heart, your will, your service,—
give yourself to Him to obey all His requirements; and you must *take* all,— Christ, the
fulness of all blessing, to abide in your heart, to
be your strength, your righteousness, your everlasting helper,— to give you power to obey."—
" *Steps to Christ,*" *pp. 69, 70.*

Thousands of people have surrendered all to
the Lord as fully as they knew how, and yet in
perplexity because of the consciousness of some
great deficiency, they cry, like the young man
who came to Christ, " What lack I yet? " Here
the difficulty is clearly pointed out. Abiding in
Christ is the result of " *giving* and *taking.*"
They may have given all with honest and sin-

cere hearts, but they have not *taken all*. There must be a constant appropriation of Christ by faith.

We need not say, " Lord, give Thyself to me," for He has already done that. But we should say, " Blessed Saviour, since Thou hast given Thyself to me, and invited me to receive Thee into my heart, I now open wide the door, and welcome Thee in. I thank Thee that Thou hast come in, and Thy presence is a reality this moment." The promise is realized as soon as we meet the conditions and claim its fulfilment.

Thus by the exercise of simple faith His indwelling is a reality in us, and in the same manner we enter into and *abide in Him*. He knows well how helpless we are to place ourselves in Him, or to keep ourselves abiding; but He says that " we are in Him that is true, even in His Son Jesus Christ," and He bids us to *abide in Him*.

Even after we have entered " the secret place of the Most High," how often we worry and fear lest we shall forget and cease to " abide under the shadow of the Almighty." Ps. 91: 1. All this hinders our progress, for we are assuming responsibility for something which only our Lord can do. He requires only what we can do, and then He promises His people, under the beautiful figure of the vineyard, " I the Lord do keep it; I will water it every moment: . . . I will keep it night and day." Isa. 27 : 3. So long as we do not neglect the simple conditions of co-operation, God will do all for and in us that is required.

" Consecrate yourself to God in the morning; make this your very first work. Let your prayer be, ' Take me, O Lord, as wholly Thine. I lay all my plans at Thy feet. Use me today in Thy service. Abide with me, and let all my work be wrought in Thee.' This is a daily matter. Each morning consecrate yourself to God for that day. Surrender all your plans to Him, to be carried out or given up as His providence shall indicate. Thus day by day you may be giving your life into the hands of God, and thus your life will be molded more and more after the life of Christ.

" A life in Christ is a life of restfulness. There may be no ecstasy of feeling, but there should be an abiding, peaceful trust. Your hope is not in yourself; it is in Christ. Your weakness is united to His strength, your ignorance to His wisdom, your frailty to His enduring might."— " Steps to Christ," p. 70.

A terrible storm is raging. The snow is falling fast, and the wind is blowing wildly. The parents have made sure that all the children are safely in the home. Then the father gives

the word, " All remain in the house." How
foolish for one child to say that he cannot abide
in the house, but must plunge into the bitter
cold, to suffer and perhaps perish! Our heavenly Father has gathered all His children into
the fold, which is Christ. He does not command
you not to go out, but He entreats you to abide
within. Christ has bidden His children to abide
in Him. God has placed us there, and will never
cast us out. No other power in the world is able
to separate us from Him, apart from our own
choice.

" When Christ took human nature upon Him,
He bound humanity to Himself by a tie of love
that can never be broken by any power save the
choice of man himself. Satan will constantly
present allurements to induce us to break this
tie,— to choose to separate ourselves from Christ.
Here is where we need to watch, to strive, to
pray, that nothing may entice us to *choose* another master; for we are always free to do this.
But let us keep our eyes fixed upon Christ, and
He will preserve us. Looking unto Jesus, we
are safe. Nothing can pluck us out of His
hand."—" *Steps to Christ*," *p. 72.*

Many worry and perplex themselves trying
to get into a state of certainty that they will
abide in Christ, and not fall again; but this is
only a waste of time, for the experience is ours

step by step. A lady met with a serious and painful accident. Her first question when the doctor came was, " Doctor, how long shall I have to lie here? " Very kindly the doctor answered, " Only one day — at a time." So each morning, as we consecrate our lives anew to Him, we may say, " Now, blessed Master, I am in Thee; teach me to abide quietly, humbly, and obediently, moment by moment. Teach me to trust Thee to keep me abiding."

What promise could the Master give· that would offer a greater inducement or a stronger appeal to seek a life of victory over sin than the promise of His near return!

" I go to prepare a place for you. And if I go and prepare a place for you, I will come again, and receive you unto Myself; that where I am, there ye may be also." John 14: 2, 3.

" Every man that hath this hope in him purifieth himself, even as He is pure." 1 John 3: 3.

Soon that glorious event will occur which will mark the end of the reign of sin, and the beginning of the reign of everlasting righteousness. Through all the ages the children of God have looked forward to the coming of the One who is to reign as King of kings and Lord of lords. From the fulfilment of the Saviour's own predictions we know that the hour draweth on apace.

"And now, little children, ABIDE IN HIM; that, when He shall appear, we may have confidence, and not be ashamed before Him at His coming." 1 John 2 : 28.

Fitted for Service

O TURN me, mold me, mellow me for use,
Pervade my being with Thy vital force,
That this else inexpressive life of mine
May become eloquent and full of power,
Impregnated with life and strength divine.
Put the bright torch of heaven into my hand,
That I may carry it aloft,
And win the eye of weary wanderers here below,
To guide their feet into the paths of peace.

I cannot raise the dead,
Nor from the soil pluck precious dust,
Nor bid the sleeper wake,
Nor still the storm, nor bend the lightning back,
Nor muffle up the thunder,
Nor bid the chains fall from off creation's long enfettered
    limbs;
But I can live a life that tells on other lives,
And makes the world less full of anguish and of pain —
A life that, like the pebble dropped upon the sea,
Sends its wide circles to a hundred shores.

May such a life be mine!
Creator of true life, Thyself the life Thou givest,
Give Thyself that Thou mayest dwell in me, and I in Thee.

— Horatius Bonar.

We'd love to have you download our catalog of
titles we publish at:

www.TEACHServices.com

or write or email us your thoughts,
reactions, or criticism about this
or any other book we publish at:

TEACH Services, Inc.
254 Donovan Road
Brushton, NY 12916

info@TEACHServices.com

or you may call us at:

518/358-3494

Produced in partnership with
LNFBooks.com

LaVergne, TN USA
14 September 2010
197012LV00004B/27/P